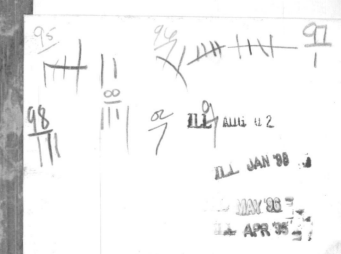

TEXT

BY

LAWRENCE W. CHEEK

PHOTOGRAPHS

BY

ARIZONA HIGHWAYS

CONTRIBUTORS

ANCIENT PEOPLES OF THE SOUTHWEST

A.D. 1250

ARIZONA
HIGHWAYS BOOK

ANASAZI

(PRECEDING PANEL) Betatakin Ruin, Navajo National Monument. Although Betatakin and Keet Seel hide in canyons less than a dozen miles from each other, Betatakin was not discovered by white men until 14 years after Keet Seel. Navajo guides led Richard and John Wetherill, the amateur archaeologist brothers who discovered the ruins at Mesa Verde, Colorado, to these premier Arizona ruins — Richard to Keet Seel in 1895, and John, accompanied by Professor Byron Cummings, to Betatakin in 1909.
DAVID MUENCH

SINAGUA

(RIGHT) Tuzigoot National Monument on the banks of the Verde River in central Arizona. Built amid ample water, fertile soil, and moderate climate, Tuzigoot blossomed in the late A.D. 1200s. The growth may have been due to migration from other Sinagua villages in the Flagstaff area where shortened growing seasons wreaked havoc on food supplies.
RANDY A. PRENTICE

MOGOLLON

(FOLLOWING PANEL) Gila Cliff Dwellings National Monument, southwestern New Mexico. The Mogollon culture, the mountain farmers of Arizona, New Mexico, and northern Mexico, built these cliff dwellings in the canyon walls near the upper reaches of the Gila River. In addition to fine quality pottery, the Mogollon were known for their turquoise necklaces, which they traded throughout the region and far south into Mexico.
RUSS FINLEY

JERRY JACKA

HOHOKAM

(LEFT) Casa Grande Ruins National Monument, central Arizona. When Jesuit missionary Father Eusebio Kino came upon the "Big House," as he named it, in 1694, he probably was the first non-Indian ever to see it. Archaeologists think Casa Grande may have been an ancient astronomical observatory. Other structures adjacent to the four-story adobe Casa Grande include common pithouses and a ceremonial ball court, all surrounded by an adobe wall. Although there was a small entrance on the north end, the Casa Grandeans entered the compound and Casa Grande by ladder. Irrigated fields surrounding the village compound produced corn, beans, squash, and cotton for the Hohokam.

TOM DANIELSEN

SALADO

(FOLLOWING PANEL) Human cultures come and go, but the beauty of the land remains. Desert marigolds bloom at Tonto National Monument, central Arizona. More than five centuries ago, the Salado culture abandoned these two cliff dwellings in the Tonto Basin east of Phoenix. Some archaeologists conjecture they migrated north to join the Hopi or east to join the Zuni Indians; others suggest they went south to Mexico; and still others claim they settled in the Salt River Valley, becoming the ancestors of today's Pima Indians.

JERRY JACKA

JERRY JACKA

WORLD TIMELINE

Jesus of Nazareth was born	B.C. 4
Roman army invaded Britain	A.D. 43
Mount Vesuvius erupted	79
Britain revolted against Rome	205
Constantinople was founded	330
Goths besieged and sacked Rome	410
Europe entered the Dark Ages	476
Black Death plague ravaged Europe	542
Mohammed was born at Mecca	570
Waterwheels used throughout Europe	700
Charlemagne became king of the Franks	768
Chinese developed gunpowder	850
Erik the Red discovered Greenland	982
Leif Ericsson landed in North America	1000
The First Crusade began	1096
Construction began on Notre Dame Cathedral	1163
Magna Carta signed by King John of England	1215
The first Inquisition	1233
The Renaissance began in Europe	1300
Hundred Years War began	1337
Columbus discovered the New World	1492

SOUTHWEST TIMELINE

100 B.C.	Archaic peoples began settling down
1 A.D.	Earliest evidence of pottery
50	Early Hohokam canal dug in Tempe
500	The bow and arrow appeared
600	Sinagua built pithouses near Flagstaff
750	Hohokam began constructing ball courts
900	Great Houses were being built in Chaco Canyon
1000	Habitation began at Oraibi and Acoma
1064	Sunset Crater erupted
1100	Chaco system reached its peak
1130	Fifty-year drought began
1150	Salado arrived in the Tonto Basin
1200	Great pueblos were constructed at Mesa Verde
1250	Mogollon built Casa Malpais
1276	Twenty-year drought began
1300	Keet Seel and Betatakin abandoned
1325	Winter-dominant moisture pattern began
1358	Flood damaged Hohokam canals
1400	Paquimé attacked and destroyed
1450	Period of abandonment almost fulfilled
1600	Apache and Navajo entered area

(COVER EMBOSSING) This maze symbol is similar to one found high on an inside wall at Casa Grande Ruins National Monument, which was built by the Hohokam in the early A.D. 1300s. For contemporary Pima and Tohono O'odham Indians it represents the house of Tcuhu, and the story of creation and Elder Brother, I'itoi. Campbell Grant, in *Rock Art of the North American Indian*, noted a similar image appears in ancient petroglyphs left by the Anasazi. The Hopi call it "Mother and Child." Studying the symbol, one notices two sets of arms: the inside set representing a child in the womb (or Mother Earth), and another set representing the mother holding a child. The maze symbolizes complex thought at many levels — creation, birth, wisdom — the journey of life.

Prepared by the Book Division of *Arizona Highways* magazine, a monthly publication of the Arizona Department of Transportation.
Hugh Harelson — Publisher
Wesley Holden — Book Editor
Robert J. Farrell and Rebecca Mong — Text Editors
Gary Bennett — Creative Director
Cindy Mackey — Production Director
Vicky Snow — Production Assistant

Library of Congress Catalog Number 93-91048
ISBN 0-916179-45-1

CONTENTS

A.D. 500

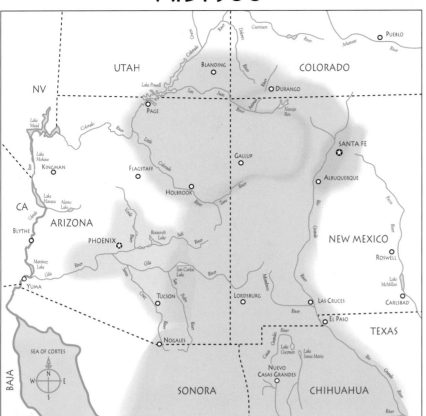

A.D. 950

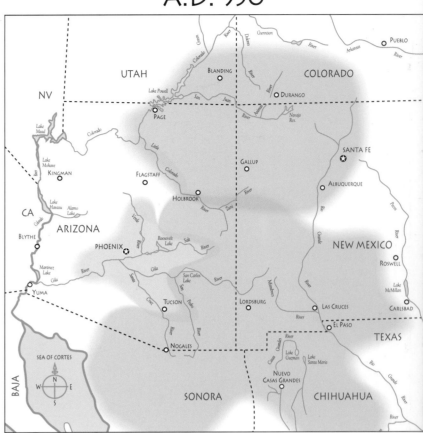

A.D. 1500

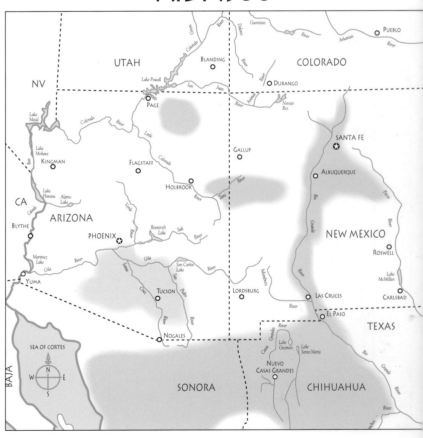

The Evolution of Prehistoric Southwest Cultures

The earliest evidence of humans in the Southwest has been radiocarbon-dated at about 11,500 years ago. Those Paleo-Indians were associated with such archaeologically famous hunting locations as the Lehner Ranch site in southeastern Arizona and Blackwater Draw near Clovis, New Mexico. The Paleo-Indians retreated eastward about 5500 B.C., and nomadic hunter-gatherers, called the Archaic Culture, moved in from the west.

Initial indications of the more sedentary Anasazi, Hohokam, and Mogollon cultures appeared shortly before A.D. 1. Like the Archaic, they were largely hunter-gatherers. Although the Archaic were the first to use corn, these new cultures depended on it even more as a supplement to their hunting-gathering diet. Indeed, the single most important event in Southwest prehistory was the recognition that corn could be a long-term storable crop.

Starting with the above map and moving in a clockwise manner, one can graphically follow the expansion, flowering, and collapse of the Anasazi, Hohokam, and Mogollon cultures as well as those of the Salado and Sinagua. While these cultures have their distinct identifying characteristics and developed in different

regions of the Southwest, they were often in contact with each other through trade and travel. As populations increased, territories overlapped, and the mixture of peoples and exchange of ideas created cultural fusions that produced communities in these regions that were so evenly mixed that they defy labeling with a singular heritage. Cliff dwellings, pueblo ruins, and other sites identified with

A.D. 1250

UTAH

NV

COLORADO

Green River

Colorado River

Dolores River

Gunnison River

Arkansas River

PUEBLO

39°

38°

BLANDING

HOVENWEEP

UTE MT.

MESA VERDE

DURANGO

37°

Lake Fowell

San Juan River

PAGE

NAVAJO

Animas River

AZTEC

Navajo Res.

River

Lake Mead

Colorado River

Little Colorado River

CANYON DE CHELLY

CHACO CANYON

BANDELIER

SANTA FE

36°

GRAND CANYON TUSAYAN

Lake Mohave

KINGMAN

WUPATKI

FLAGSTAFF

HOMOLOVI

GALLUP

CORONADO

PETROGLYPH

ALBUQUERQUE

35°

Lake Havasu

TUZIGOOT

WALNUT CANYON

HOLBROOK

PETRIFIED FOREST PUERCO

River

EL MORRO ATSINA

Pecos River

CA

Alamo Lake

MONTEZUMA CASTLE

River

Zuni River

ARIZONA

Verde River

CASA MALPAIS

NEW MEXICO

34°

BLYTHE

Colorado River

Roosevelt Lake

Salt River

River

PHOENIX

PUEBLO GRANDE

TONTO

BESH-BA-GOWAH

GILA CLIFF DWELLINGS

25

Rio Grande

ROSWELL

Martinez Lake

River

Gila

Gila River

San Carlos Lake

River

CASA GRANDE

San Pedro River

Mimbres River

33°

Lake McMillan

YUMA

Santa Cruz River

TUCSON

LORDSBURG

LAS CRUCES

CARLSBAD

River

E. PASO

32°

NOGALES

River

TEXAS

Grandes River

Casas Grandes River

Lake Guzman

Lake Santa Maria

Rio Grande

31°

BAJA

SEA OF CORTES

NUEVO CASAS GRANDES

SONORA

CASAS GRANDES PAQUIME

CHIHUAHUA

30°

114°   113°   112°   111°   110°   109°   108°   107°   106°   105°   104°

these cultures appear on the A.D. 1250 map. The approximate relationships of interstate highways, some modern cities, major streams and rivers, and latitude and longitude lines are included as reference points. Most of the sites are national parks or monuments, while others are operated by a state, a city, or an Indian tribe. All are open to the public.

LEGEND

PARK OR MONUMENT   INTERSTATE ROUTES

STATE CAPITAL   OTHER CITIES

ANASAZI   SALADO

MOGOLLON   SINACUA

HOHOKAM

MAPS BY W. RANDALL IRVINE

15

A.D. 1250

INTRODUCTION

On the written calendar of a distant continent, it is A.D. 1250, the High Middle Ages. England has just seen the dawn of the Magna Carta, and in Rome the church has launched the Inquisition. The European air clouds with promise and trepidation.

In the unwritten history of the ancient cultures of the American Southwest, A.D. 1250 is also the midpoint of a tumultuous century. In the desert, people gradually have been abandoning their more primitive pithouses for adobe condominiums enclosed by compound walls, one of many architectural hints

of a changing social or political order. On the Colorado Plateau, the Sinagua are dying off or scattering, while nearby the Anasazi are building breathtakingly dramatic pueblos in the sheltering natural alcoves of canyon walls. In the Chihuahuan desert south of the modern border with Mexico, another people is operating an astounding Mesoamerican-like trading center complete with high-rise adobe towers and municipal water and sewer systems never before seen in this land. But in about 10 years this prehistoric city, for no reason readily apparent today, will begin its slide toward oblivion.

Nearly everywhere the arts of architecture, pottery, textiles, and jewelry have reached their expressive peak. Religious ceremonies are more complex and vital than ever, perhaps because people feel increasingly dependent on the benevolence of the spirits that manage the environment. Cultures are more advanced but, ironically, less secure. By A.D. 1250, the upward population curve is about to overtake these cultures' knowledge about wresting a living from the land.

...DISCOVERING A PLACE IN THE SUN

Human effigies in stone and clay provide glimpses of what the ancients may have looked like. **(ABOVE)** This tiny 2 5/8-inch-tall painted Anasazi figurine of modeled clay was found near Springerville in eastern Arizona. Its sculptured form shows what may be ceremonial body painting and a worshipful pose. **(RIGHT, CLOCKWISE FROM TOP, LEFT)** A carved stone effigy from the Sinagua culture near Flagstaff stands six inches tall and has a flattened visage with a heavy brow. A pottery face from the Mogollon culture may illustrate body paint or tattoos. This Tonto Basin polychrome effigy vessel from the Salado culture sports pendant earrings. The swirl design on this Hohokam red-on-buff effigy pot may depict a hairdo as well as face painting.

PHOTOGRAPHS BY JERRY JACKA

Distinctively different styles of pottery and their decoration, or lack of it, provide trademarks for each culture.

(ABOVE) An Anasazi polychrome bowl from the White Mountains of eastern Arizona displays bold, loosely drawn geometric designs.
GEORGE H.H. HUEY

(BELOW) A whimsical water bird cavorts across a red-on-buff Hohokam plate.
JERRY JACKA

(ABOVE) Undecorated brownware was the common pottery of the Sinagua culture.
RICHARD WESTON

(ABOVE) A Mogollon black-on-white bowl features precise pin-striping, cross-hatching, and a stylized fish. As with nearly all of their bowls, this one has a hole punched through the center.
JERRY JACKA

(BELOW) This Salado polychrome olla displays the classic shape and exquisitely painted geometric designs that made this style of pottery one of the most highly valued and widely traded in the prehistoric Southwest.
GEORGE H.H. HUEY

The environment is stressed; large numbers of people are competing for dwindling natural resources. Tensions are tightening under the cloud of potential starvation. People are clustering in larger and larger settlements, believing that safety and survival lie in numbers. In a few years, two disastrous climatic changes will force a widespread dispersion from traditional homelands. First there will be a severe generation-long drought, then a seemingly endless series of long, stubborn winters and concurrent shorter summers in which to try coaxing crops to maturity.

One to two centuries later, the heartbeats of early Southwest cultures are found in widely different places. The Anasazi, Hohokam, Salado, Mogollon, and Sinagua no longer exist as distinct peoples. The refugees have merged into complex cultural blends. Among the many tribal names are those we now call Tohono O'odham (Papago), Akimel O'odham (Pima), and Hopi in Arizona; and Zuni, Acoma, and the other Pueblo tribes of New Mexico's Rio Grande Valley. In the deserts of Arizona and northern Mexico the population has shriveled, and where it survives, most people eke out marginal lives.

Questions crackle like sparks from a campfire. Where did these prehistoric cultures come from? Speaking different languages and embracing different religious traditions, how, and why, did they get along — particularly after a hostile environment began to squeeze them? How did they thrive for so long in the beautiful but implacable badlands of the Southwest's deserts, plateaus, and canyons? And do the answers hold lessons for our own civilization, which now occupies the same fragile lands? Or indeed are there answers for an overcrowded world?

Archaeology is digging into these questions — sometimes the answers come up short, sometimes intriguingly fulfilling.

In the American Southwest, archaeology is barely a century old. Beginning in the 1880s, pioneers such as Frank Cushing, Gustaf Nordenskiold, Adolph Bandelier, and Richard Wetherill discovered and excavated a parade of ruins that kept them in a state of continual astonishment. None of these men was a trained archaeologist; Cushing and Nordenskiold were both naturalists, Bandelier had been trained as a geologist, and Wetherill was a cowboy. They all learned on the job.

Wetherill's story illustrates the enchanting attraction of this prehistoric terra incognita. In 1888 he was combing a canyon in southwestern Colorado for stray cattle when he glanced up and saw an immense Anasazi pueblo huddled in an alcove. "The solemn grandeur of the outlines was breathtaking," he wrote later. These are hardly cowboy words, and Wetherill was hardly a cowboy after discovering the ruin he named Cliff Palace. He spent the rest of

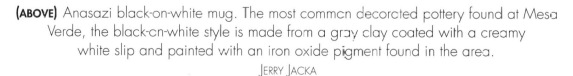

(ABOVE) Anasazi black-on-white mug. The most common decorated pottery found at Mesa Verde, the black-on-white style is made from a gray clay coated with a creamy white slip and painted with an iron oxide pigment found in the area.
JERRY JACKA

(FOLLOWING PANEL) Cliff Palace, Mesa Verde National Park, southwestern Colorado. With an average 18 inches of annual precipitation, the Anasazi of Mesa Verde were able to dry farm on the mesa tops. They reached their fields by climbing the steep cliffs using handholds and footholds chopped into the sandstone.
DAVID MUENCH

his life digging into antiquity.

It wasn't until the early 20th century that Southwestern archaeology acquired the tool it needed to become a real science. In 1904 an Arizona astronomer named Andrew E. Douglass began trying to reconstruct past climates by measuring tree rings. He suspected a link to sunspot cycles. By 1919 he had invented the science of dendrochronology, which not only provided a historic record of year-to-year precipitation, but also a method of dating a piece of wood by comparing its ring pattern with known samples. Dendrochronology proved to be much more of a boon to archaeology than to astronomy. For the first time, archaeologists could chart sequences of events, dating the exact year that wood was cut by an Anasazi family to build a home or roast a rabbit. And the information about ancient cycles of drought and plenty helped archaeologists craft assumptions about prehistoric social behavior.

Since then, the science of archaeology has developed many more

investigative tools. They ponder oral histories and myths of modern Indians as possible windows on the past. They use what are called "ethnographic analogies," studying how modern non-industrialized people hunt, garden, and govern themselves to infer how prehistoric Southwesterners might have done the same things. Biochemical analysis of plant pollen and human bones provides profiles of diets, diseases, and the environment.

Some archaeologists are fond of what might be called "common-sense archaeology." When the spring in your canyon dries up, you leave — and perhaps, if you notice that the creek in another canyon is poorly defended, you attack and claim it. This seems like simple human nature. But others are decidedly leery of "common sense" because "common" modern behavior is firmly rooted in a background of European culture instead of Southwest Indian culture.

Despite all the science that has been focused on it, much of Southwestern prehistory

22

remains cloudy and ambiguous. The army of questions overwhelms the supply of answers. And the answers keep shifting; each new investigative technique yields new information that may overturn old interpretations. There still are not enough techniques available; archaeologists admit that their picture of prehistoric cultures here is stitched together with assumptions and inferences. They argue collegially but endlessly, studying the same evidence and extracting radically different conclusions. Southwestern prehistory is a connect-the-dots puzzle in which not enough dots exist to make a complete picture. And in which, every few moments, the dots keep shifting to change even the fragments.

Humans have lived in the American Southwest for about 11,500 years. When they first arrived here, the Ice Age had ended and the climate was wetter and cooler than it is today. The Sonoran and Chihuahuan deserts were then grasslands, grazed not only by mammoth but other big mammals extinct in the region today: mastodon, bison, camel, and tapir. The saber-toothed tiger, fortunately for the Paleo-Indians, was already extinct. Although relatively little is known about the first 9,000 years, one pivotal discovery helps explain how archaeology works.

In 1952 a southeastern Arizona rancher named Ed Lehner spotted a cache of bones sticking out of the bank of an arroyo. Lehner knew immediately they were too large to be bones of modern animals, so he contacted Emil Haury, the eminent University of Arizona archaeologist. Haury supervised an excavation, which eventually turned up the remains of nine mammoths with 13 spearpoints lodged among their bones, various cutting and chopping tools, and two cooking fires. Lehner's ranch had been a prehistoric killing field.

By radiocarbon dating the bones and charcoal, archaeologists pegged the date of the kill at about 9000 B.C. The multiple spearpoints confirmed that these primitive men, the Paleo-Indians, hunted in concert. The remains of multiple animals showed that they hunted herds of mammoths. Checking the social behavior of the mammoth's nearest modern relative, the elephant, archaeologists noted that herds consist of matriarchal cows that do not scatter, but form a protective circle around their calves when they sense danger. By inference, so did herds of mammoths. It must have seemed efficient to these ancient hunters to kill an entire herd at once: the meat would have fed a lot of hungry people and would have attracted more game as other carnivores came to feast on the carrion. But it was a self-defeating strategy because it eventually exhausted the supply of reproducing cows and ultimately led to mammoth extinction.

Paleo-Indians lived in small wandering groups of 25 to perhaps 75 people. They did not build permanent shelters, cultivate crops, or make pottery. Apparently they had some concept of a

(LEFT) Eleven thousand years ago, a Paleo-Indian hunting party killed nine woolly mammoths at a place now called Lehner Kill Site, along the San Pedro River in southeastern Arizona.
ILLUSTRATION BY GARY BENNETT
(ABOVE) One of the 13 Clovis-style spear points found among the giant mammoth bones.
JERRY JACKA

Stone knives and projectile points (spearpoints and arrowheads) were usually made from glasslike chert or chalcedony which breaks off in razor-sharp edges.

(ABOVE, AND LEFT) These points were roughed out from the core stone (here, chert) using the percussion method of breaking off small pieces with a hammer stone that was harder than the core. A suitable piece would then be further worked until ready for the final stage.
(BOTTOM LEFT) A deer or elk antler was then used to exert pressure against the edges, flaking off small pieces until the stone reached its final shape with sharply notched, well-defined edges.

PHOTOGRAPHS BY JERRY JACKA

Prehistoric Southwestern cultures used a variety of stone knives and projectile points. They range in size from 11/16 inches to 2 3/4 inches. **(TOP ROW, LEFT TO RIGHT)** The Anasazi made these brown and red chert bifacial knives. Two Basketmaker (pre-Anasazi) white chert dart points probably were used with atlatls. A Salado red jasper point and four Hohokam chalcedony and chert points were made for arrows. A chert drill typical of those used throughout the Southwest. **(BOTTOM ROW, LEFT TO RIGHT)** Two Anasazi points, obsidian and chalcedony; and seven obsidian, yellow jasper, and white chert were from the central Arizona Hohokam and Salado cultures.

(ABOVE) Early archers straightened their arrow shafts with a notched stone heated in a fire. The arrow's shaft was held in the groove of the hot stone until the warming of the sap made the wood more flexible. The shaft was then removed and held straight until it cooled.

spirit world: like far more sophisticated people would do in the Southwest 10,000 years later, they buried tools with their dead.

By around 5500 B.C. the climate had dried and warmed, and the large game animals retreated east to better grazing. The Paleo-Indians followed. Some Paleo-descendants may have become part of a second Southwestern people, the Archaic or Desert Culture, as they moved in from the west and elsewhere.

The Archaic people also were nomadic hunter-gatherers, but they made use of a larger constellation of wild plants and meats than their predecessors. They also had one vitally important bit of technology that the Paleo-Indians had lacked until the latter part of their time: the food processor (a mano and metate, or stone grinder). This innovation thus became part of the most profound change in all North American history: agriculture.

Common-sense archaeology assumes that Paleo-Indian and Archaic lives were short and hard, but common sense may be wrong. As long as game was plentiful, hunter-gatherers spent less time making their living — getting the food they needed to survive — than agriculturists. Their diet was more varied and richer in protein, and because they only counted on native plants and animals, they didn't have to worry about crop failure in dry years. The lives of the prehistoric Southwestern farmers, who would appear thousands of years later, were vastly more complicated and tenuous. Some anthropologists think humans took up farming as a last resort, only after their population had over-

whelmed the truly natural resources. Others disagree.

Here is why: one person per square mile can live by Archaic techniques. Agriculture can support five to 10 people per square mile. The intensity of the latter provides more food, but limits the old practices of wide-range food gathering. So which came first? An increased population that provided the manpower to cultivate more food, or more food that allowed the population to increase — it's a chicken-and-egg puzzle.

Corn had been cultivated in central

Desert harvest. The Archaic hunter-gatherers of central and southern Arizona relied solely on the natural bounty of the land. Their descendants, the Hohokam and Salado who farmed corn, beans, and squash, depended on the natural desert foods for as much as 60 percent of their diet.
(ABOVE) Some varieties of Sonoran desert foods are from top left, mesquite beans; top right, the beans ground into meal; left center, fruit of two varieties of prickly pear cactus; lower left, saguaro fruit; lower right, several types of dried wild beans.
JERRY JACKA
(LEFT) A Sinagua stone ax with its original bent cottonwood handle.
GEORGE H.H. HUEY

The Sinagua spent most of their time out-of-doors, but some activities, such as corn grinding, took place
almost exclusively inside. This idealized re-creation of Sinagua living quarters at Tuzigoot National
Monument museum provides a look at the small but comfortable room where a Sinagua family would have
slept and congregated in bad weather. A metate and mano for grinding corn are on the floor. At left stands
a loom for weaving cotton that was traded from the Hohokam farmers to the south. Right is a rack for
treating animal hides. A macaw, perhaps imported from Casas Grandes, Mexico, perches on the ladder.
The feathers of these birds were used for decoration and ceremonial purposes.

JERRY JACKA

The staple of the prehistoric Southwesterner's diet, the hardy multicolored corn.
JERRY JACKA

Prehistoric corn grinding methods took many shapes. **(ABOVE)** Three adjoining stone boxes at Keet Seel allowed for neighborly conversation while grinding corn into coarse, medium, and fine meal.
RUSS FINLEY

(RIGHT) A prehistoric bedrock mortar at Phoenix' South Mountain.
JERRY JACKA

28

Corn cobs such as these from Tonto National Monument were found at numerous ruins throughout the region.
P.K. Weis

Residents of Mesa Verde's Step House Ruin found the stone surface outside their pueblo door provided a serviceable surface for milling corn.
Tom Till

The classic metate and mano from the Salado culture of central Arizona.
Jerry Jacka

Mexico since at least 5000 B.C. By 1000 B.C., possibly earlier, a primitive corn made its debut north of the present-day border, introduced by migrants or traders. Its impact was negligible at first. It was planted sporadically, and watering was left to the whims of the spirits. Gradually, as more and more productive varieties were introduced, corn transformed cultures. As archaeologist Alfred E. Dittert points out, the single most important event in the prehistory of the Southwest was the recognition that corn could be a long-term storable crop. A surplus of corn made it possible to subsist even when no wild foods were fruiting nearby. As a result, social organization became larger and more complex.

To make year-round use of grains, people needed storage systems — hence, pits, then basketry, then pottery. To cultivate fields, they had to have permanent settlements — which meant the dawn of architecture, then planning and government. To promote successful crops they employed a keen knowledge of plants, soils, and their environments, and practiced elaborate religions. Just as early European history cannot be discussed without the mention of Christianity, so did religion play a prominent role in the life of prehistoric Southwesterners. Today's Hopi, Zuni, and other Pueblo peoples continue to perform kachina ceremonies, permitting anthropologists to infer the cultural fabric of times past.

These are the elements that shaped Southwestern cultures from the beginning of the Christian era to A.D. 1250.

Like other books on the prehistoric Southwest, this one can only be a snapshot of a scene that is still changing, chameleonlike, as new light falls on it. The difference is that a journalist and not a scientist is writing here, and the journalist is more willing to crawl out on that rain-slick limb and to tell what he knows in plain English.

This book introduces what we know about the peoples who claimed this land before the Spaniards arrived in A.D. 1540 with guns, horses, and a written language. It provides a practical guide to the most important ruins and archaeological museums in the Southwest. And for anyone captivated by mystery, it may be a portal to a lifetime obsession.

In addition to the hundreds of books and papers I read before beginning this two-and-a-half-year project, every park and monument mentioned in this book was visited, and more than a score of archaeologists were interviewed. Several read early versions of this manuscript and offered suggestions. The final product, however, is my own and the editors of *Arizona Highways*.

Ancient farmers of the Southwest used various containers for storing corn, from pits to baskets to pottery. Here archaeologist Tom Bodor records information on a granary at a Tonto Basin ruin.
JERRY JACKA

Lawrence W. Cheek

Lawrence W. Cheek was born and raised in the Southwest. He lives on the outskirts of Tucson, a quarter-mile away from a prehistoric Hohokam village. Through the years he has written countless articles, been an editor, and taught journalism.
He has authored two other books published by *Arizona Highways*, *Scenic Sedona* and *Photographing Arizona*.

CHAPTER ONE

ANASAZI

...STONEMASONS OF THE COLORADO PLATEAU

Somewhere in Chaco Canyon, New Mexico, a coyote calls in the dawn, its virtuosic yodel rebounding for miles along the chasm's sandstone walls. Long moments pass. There is no reply, only silence. And silence in Chaco Canyon is like silence on the moon.

At the same time, a solitary human walks slowly across the long shadows in the ruin of Chaco's Pueblo Bonito, one of the eeriest remnants of the prehistoric world in the land we now call North America. The coyote's unreturned call strikes the visitor as a metaphor for his own meditations. There are few answers for us modern-day humans in the ruins of Chaco Canyon. But the questions are countless.

What was Chaco? Competing theories rise and fall, like skyrockets crossing paths in the night. Was it a religious and ceremonial center, a prehistoric Mecca? Was it an authoritarian city-state, like Athens a millennium earlier or Moscow a millennium later, ruling the region around it and extracting tribute? Or was Chaco an urban experiment destined to fail because it attracted too many hungry and thirsty mouths to a land poorly equipped to nourish them?

The great pueblos of Chaco Canyon were built by the Anasazi, a culture whose remnants are scattered across four states — Arizona, New Mexico, Colorado, and Utah. Their achievements in agriculture, art, and particularly architecture inspire profound respect today among both casual visitors and professional archaeologists. Chaco Canyon is only one of countless Anasazi settlements, and while it is the most baffling, all of them are enchanting.

The Navajo, who filtered into the abandoned Anasazi landscape in the 1500s, provided the people's name. Often blandly rendered as "the ancient ones," Anasazi is better translated as "enemy ancestors."

Early archaeologists were captivated by these ruins, however, and as the result of more than a century of intensive research we now know more about the Anasazi than any other prehistoric culture of the Southwest. "Culture," however, should perhaps be pluralized. The Anasazi were not a monolithic ethnic group. So many differences characterize their architecture and art that archaeologists suspect they even spoke several different languages.

(PRECEDING PAGE 31)
This painted modeled clay Anasazi effigy figure stands 2 5/8 inches tall.
JERRY JACKA

(LEFT) Chacoan stonemasons performed exceptional work following a style that used small, closely fitted stones with thin mortar joints. It has been suggested by some that T-shaped doorways designated rooms with special religious or ceremonial significance.
LAURENCE PARENT
(ABOVE) In the buff sandstone walls of Aztec Ruin, northwest of Chaco, Anasazi stonemasons laid decorative layers of green stone.
JEFF GNASS
(FOLLOWING PANEL) An aerial view of Pueblo Bonito, one of the great houses at Chaco Canyon. At the base of this arid plateau, with little reliable water nearby, the Anasazi built the grand religious and political power center of their culture.
TOM TILL

Their descendants, the Pueblo Indians of Arizona and New Mexico, today speak six distinctly different languages.

The earliest Anasazi were Archaic people who, around 100 B.C., began to give up their nomadic wandering and settle down to a mixed life of hunting, gathering, and "farming." Archaeologists call these people "Basketmakers" for their finely woven yucca-fiber baskets. In the beginning their only crops were corn and squash, probably introduced by itinerants from Mesoamerica (southern Mexico and Central America). Beans would not appear until after A.D. 500, and the domestication of turkeys came still later.

Corn, beans, and squash had been cultivated in Mesoamerica since possibly 5,000 B.C. It may seem strange that it took several millennia for the concept of agriculture to travel less than 2,000 miles, but there are plausible reasons. The Sonoran and Chihuahuan deserts, which separate Mesoamerica from the Colorado Plateau, would have been a formidable barrier to cross; Central American refugees still die trying it in modern times. The Anasazi landscape, with its short growing seasons and as little as eight inches of rainfall a year, may have looked like a poor prospect for cultivation. Or maybe the Archaics, few in number and blessed for a long time with plentiful game, saw no point in going into the corn business until increasing population forced it upon them.

Even after the Basketmakers began growing some of their food, technological progress came slowly. They hunted with spears and atlatls, wooden levers that extended the throwing arm's radius to launch the missiles with greater velocity. They lived in pithouses in which a floor would be excavated about 20 inches below ground level and a framework of poles, sticks, and mud mortar heaped over it. Typically the dwellings were about 15 feet in diameter, although some startlingly large rooms up to 47 feet across and six feet deep have been found. These were communal kivas or dwellings for extended families.

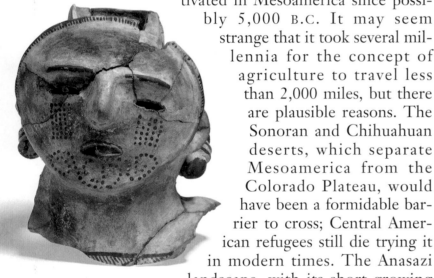

Generally the pithouses had no doors; residents entered through openings in the roofs.

Probably the transition from hunting and gathering to greater dependence on agriculture was slow, halting, and ever controversial, but the very "idea" that corn was a storable food is the single most important event in Southwest prehistory.

Pottery logically follows agriculture because it provides a means for the efficient storage and cooking of grains. In the world of the Basketmaker it appeared about A.D. 200. The bow and arrow probably appeared in the Anasazi arsenal between 500 and 700, and finally, pueblo stone architecture appeared beside pithouses beginning around 750. These three developments took nearly five hundred years to pervade Anasazi life, but together, they revolutionized it.

In the beginning, pottery was not an expressive art form, but simply a marvelous new kitchen implement. Early Basketmaker yucca-fiber baskets were sometimes so tightly woven that they could hold water. The only way to cook in them was to drop fire-heated stones in with the grains or beans — a slow, tedious, and probably hazardous process. Clay pots could be heated directly over a fire, resting on stones or lumps of clay. A covered pot used for storing grain, unlike a fiber basket, would repel the assaults of rodents and insects.

When bows and arrows arrived, they enlarged the Anasazi menu as well as their survival skills, supplementing the old spears, traps, and snares. In the hands of a skilled hunter, a spear can bring down a deer or antelope but not a bird or rodent. The bow and arrow brought a new dimension to Anasazi hunting.

The gradual transition from pithouse to pueblo architecture may have occurred for several reasons. The more the Anasazi came to depend on agriculture, the more they needed well-built storage rooms that could protect food from mildew, insects, and burrowing vermin — and possibly human burglars. And, beginning about A.D. 750, the replacement of single-family dwellings with blocks of connected rooms is a sign that the concept of clans, semi-autonomous groups related by kinship, was evolving in Anasazi society.

One other debatable reason for this architectural revolution occurs to modern visitors who invite aching muscles or an attack of acrophobia by climbing into one of the canyon aeries that became common after A.D. 1100: Anasazi cliff dwellings were designed for defense.

Early explorers were certain of it. In 1884 journalist Charles Lummis explored a number of canyon pueblos and concluded instinctively that the Anasazi were "patient, industrious, home-loving farmers, but harassed eternally by wily and merciless savages." In Arizona's Canyon de Chelly, Lummis observed "[the Pueblos] are usually high up from the bottom of the cliff, and between them and the foot is a precipitous ascent which no enemy could scale if any resistance whatever were made." Nine years later Swedish-born Gustaf Nordenskiold similarly theorized that ". . . nothing short of the ever imminent attacks of a hostile people can have driven the cliff-dwellers to these impregnable mountain fastnesses . . . ."

If "hostile people" were about, the threat apparently intensified over time. In A.D. 950 only 20 percent of the people of Mesa Verde lived in the canyon; the rest remained on the mountaintop in the open. By 1150, 66 percent of the Mesa Verdeans were huddling in the canyon to the south. Most of the great cliff dwellings throughout the region were built in the 1200s.

Opponents of this theory, meanwhile, point out that the entire valley on the north side of the mesa had a larger population than on the mesa. They had no defensive structures or topographic advantages for protection, and the valley's time of occupation, A.D. 500 to 1300, corresponded approximately to that of Mesa Verde.

What appeared obvious to Lummis and Nordenskiold is highly controversial today. Few topics are more likely to start

(RIGHT) This petroglyph, perhaps of a hunter, was pecked into the stone after A.D. 500. Prior to the introduction of the bow and arrow, hunters used spears, atlatls, snares, and traps.
WESLEY HOLDEN

Prehistoric baskets predated pottery, and the Anasazi wove some of the finest. Because of the abundance and quality of their baskets, Richard Wetherill, discoverer of Mesa Verde and numerous other Anasazi ruins, named the early Anasazi the "Basketmakers."

(CLOCKWISE FROM TOP) An exceptional example of an Anasazi basket bowl found in southwestern Utah, woven between A.D. 400 and 800. Detail of a basket with painted animal designs from Antelope House, Arizona. An unusually shaped bifurcated basket. A woven pouch which contained dried corn and corn meal, and a small painted basket.
ALL BY JERRY JACKA

a debate among archaeologists than mention of prehistoric Southwestern warfare. Many argue that the interpretation of "impregnable mountain fastnesses" represents a European concept of siege and defense that was never known to native Americans of the Southwest.

Whatever their motivation, the late Pueblo Anasazi created some of the most captivating architecture ever to appear in North America. Hundreds of years later, Frank Lloyd Wright would devise a philosophy of "organic architecture," in which a building grows naturally and inevitably from its site, like an extension of Nature itself. Yet Wright himself never designed anything quite as organic as Anasazi cliff dwellings. Another great American architect, Louis Sullivan, wrote in 1896 that "Form ever follows function." But the Anasazi forms expressed their function more convincingly than Sullivan's ever did.

The best-preserved ruins, such as Cliff Palace in Colorado and Keet Seel in Arizona, lie in natural alcoves of sandstone canyon walls, where they enjoy shelter from rain and snow. Generally they open to the south to take advantage of solar heating in winter, while remaining in the alcove's shade during summer's hottest days. Although there are many styles of Anasazi masonry, the pueblos usually are built of sandstone shaped into rectangular blocks and laid up with clay mortar. Ornamentation is rare, but a few pueblos, such as Aztec in New Mexico, sport bands of different-colored blocks set in outside walls. Inside, rooms usually were plastered and, on rare occasions, painted symbols are found on them too.

By modern standards, Anasazi living quarters were dark and small. A typical pueblo room might be eight by 10 feet with a ceiling less than seven feet high. There were usually no windows, just a doorway so low that one would have had to stoop to enter. Again, it is hazardous to contemplate Anasazi architecture through the lenses of European cultural conditioning. To the Anasazi, "indoors" was for food processing, storage, sleeping, occasionally for cooking, and a refuge during bad weather. Their "living room" was the outdoors.

One curiosity of pueblo architecture is the T-shaped door, a feature that has inspired decades of archaeological speculation. One theory is that the wide upper section could be blocked with a deerskin or other covering, turning the narrow lower section into a small ventilation duct for the fireplace. Another is that the wide opening would have facilitated carrying wide loads such as bundles of firewood into the dwelling. An exotic idea is that the form echoes the Mesoamerican water deity Tlaloc, whose T-like image surfaces in many Pan-American cultures. The uniquely shaped entrance is typically found, it has been suggested, only with rooms associated with certain ceremonial functions.

Most Anasazi pueblos had several kivas, underground rooms customarily circular in shape with a central fire pit, ventilator shaft, draft deflector, and stone-bench seating integrated into the wall. A hole in the floor called a *sipapu* in Pueblo theology symbolizes the route of mankind's emergence into this world. Kivas probably were centers for sacred ceremonies and were also used for men's day-to-day clan activities.

(FACING PAGE) Keet Seel Ruin at Navajo National Monument is the largest Anasazi ruin in Arizona. Richard Wetherill, amateur archaeologist and discoverer of numerous Anasazi sites, had been told by the Navajos of a large cliff dwelling off Tsegi Canyon. He searched in vain until his mule slipped its hobbles one night and wandered away from camp. While tracking the animal, Wetherill found the magnificent ruin. A number of the doors there had been sealed, and inside Wetherill found pottery and stored corn that had been left behind nearly 500 years before, as if the Anasazi planned to return some day. RICK ODELL

(RIGHT) Exceptional weaving decorates an Anasazi cradleboard from Antelope House Ruin in Canyon de Chelly. JERRY JACKA

The Anasazi used a variety of construction techniques in building their villages.
(CLOCKWISE FROM TOP, LEFT) A reconstructed early Anasazi pithouse at Step House Ruin, Mesa Verde National Park. These simple, well-insulated dwellings were built by digging an 18-inch-deep hole and setting four posts in the floor to support the roof and side beams. Next came a lathwork of sticks covered by a layer of dirt that hardened after a rain. The opening in the roof served as an entry as well as a smoke hole. GEORGE H.H. HUEY
The great kiva at Chetro Ketl Ruin, Chaco Culture National Historic Park. Located in the center plaza of a pueblo, the kiva, Hopi for "world below," is a ceremonial chamber adapted and refined from the pithouse. The great kivas at Chaco and Aztec are typical of this design. LARRY ULRICH.
Rungs of ladders and lath on roof beams were often secured by lashing a crosspiece atop them. FRANK ZULLO
Classic viga (beam) and latilla (wooden crosspiece) ceiling at Aztec Ruins National Monument. TOM TILL
At Keet Seel, several walls are made in the jacal style in which sticks are fastened vertically against a top support beam and plastered with mud. GEORGE H.H. HUEY

A great kiva is different primarily in size. It exudes a sensation of architectural grace with an undercurrent of spiritual mystery not unlike a cathedral. In *The First American*, C.W. Ceram wrote of the reconstructed great kiva at Aztec Pueblo: "Entering this dimly lit room today, it is impossible not to feel its solemnity." The great kiva of Casa Rinconada in Chaco Canyon measures 64 feet in diameter and includes antechambers, stairways to the surface, and small crypts in the interior wall that might have held religious symbols, not unlike the stations of the cross in a Roman Catholic church.

Usually undecorated and strictly functional, a single Anasazi apartment is not much of an achievement. The pueblo of which it is a part, however, is a monumental work of art. Anasazi architecture expressed the community's character, not the individual's. Mesa Verde's Cliff Palace is the paragon. Architecture historian Vincent Scully called it "a delirium of manmade geometry," a perfect description. Kivas pock the lip of the alcove, and behind them irregularly angled apartments jostle and collide. At the back erupts a skyline of three- and four-story towers. This is architecture of incredible grace, fluidity, and audacity, disciplined by its confining site.

Anasazi pottery evolved alongside architecture, moving from crude and simply functional to graceful and elaborate. Ceramic fragments of plain brownware have been dated as far back as A.D. 200, possibly the influence (or the work) of Mogollon potters in the forests to the south of the Anasazi. Simple painted designs began to appear around 700. By the 1100s and 1200s the Anasazi were crafting pots, bowls, and mugs in dazzling variety. Each Anasazi region developed a distinctive style of decoration, which archaeologists today use to trace patterns of migration.

There were no potter's wheels in Anasazi times (nor do modern Pueblo Indians use them). Ceramics were and are still formed by the coil-and-scrape system. Coils of wet clay are layered and pinched into the rough shape of a bowl or pot, then a piece of gourd rind, or an old pottery shard, is used for scraping

(LEFT)
The reconstructed great kiva at Aztec Ruins National Monument. Much of the design of the kiva was highly symbolic. The four columns that support the roof (originally pine logs) reflect the four directions and were placed upon a stack of four large flat stones which were not just foundations for pillars, but represented the four worlds common to Pueblo belief. Some of those stones are now visible in the background.
TOM TILL

and smoothing it into final form for painting and firing.

Anasazi potters also grasped a useful principle of thermodynamics. Utilitarian cooking pots were often made with pinched, corrugated coils, which exposed more of the clay's surface area to the fire and heated the pot's contents more efficiently. Many ceramics for storage or ceremonial use were elaborately painted, usually in tense geometric abstractions of checkerboards, triangles, diamonds, zigzags, chevrons, spirals, and mazes. Occasionally animal, spirit, or human figures appeared. Early Anasazi pottery usually featured black designs on a clay that fired gray-white, but by the A.D. 1100s polychrome pottery of red-orange, black, and white was in vogue. Artistic skill varied widely among potters, of course, but the best Anasazi artists painted with such an exacting hand that the lines look almost as if engraved by a laser.

More than one student of archaeology has proposed that these designs were not whims, but that there was a commonality of symbol use. Each symbol, it is suggested, had meaning, and together on a vessel they told a complex story. This idea is controversial, and the meaning(s) of a specific symbol provokes endless debate. But the idea that potters were communicating in a shared, possibly even intercultural, symbolic language is likely.

The Anasazi also developed an advanced textile art, weaving decorated baskets, bags, sandals, and clothing from cotton, yucca fiber, or hair from dogs and humans. The museum at Mesa Verde National Park displays an astounding collection of gray and brown sashes woven from dog hair, probably used to cinch loose skins or robes. One is beautifully ornamented with a repeating diamond pattern, as elegant as anything in a Santa Fe boutique today.

Thanks to Arizona's dry climate, we know something about Anasazi music, that most evanescent of prehistoric arts. Wood flutes in playable condition have been found in dry caves in northern Arizona. Their scale is

The Anasazi dyed cotton with vegetal dyes and wove it into fine cloth used for clothing such as this kilt from Aztec Ruins National Monument.
FRANK ZULLO

(TOP) Polychrome parrot effigy excavated from Sikyatki Ruin.
(ABOVE) A St. Johns style polychrome bowl found in eastern Arizona.
BOTH BY JERRY JACKA

A Kayenta style black-on-white olla found at Navajo National Monument.
GEORGE H.H. HUEY

A#, C, C#, D, F, G, A — a strange and haunting series of notes that to modern ears seems maddeningly inconclusive. Improvise a tune on this scale, and it never comes to an end that will satisfy our ears. Anasazi music probably was associated with dance and ritual. Kokopelli, the humpbacked flute player, appears at innumerable Anasazi rock-art sites (as well as in the art of other cultures), and he frequently strikes a dancing pose. Kokopelli has many interpretations; he may have been a fertility figure or a symbolic medicine man wandering among tribes, making music and mediating disputes.

A pictograph (painting on rock) of two dancing flute players, Canyon de Chelly.
DAVID MUENCH

The riddle of Kokopelli seems small, however, compared to the great enigma of the northwestern New Mexico desert. Everyone studying Anasazi culture eventually has to confront Chaco Canyon, and this is where the windows into prehistory turn dark. Chaco is a very strange place.

It would be difficult to locate a less enchanting site for a town anywhere on the Colorado Plateau. The dominant plants are drab rabbitbrush, black greasewood, and saltbush; and the wide, shallow canyon offers no sheltering alcoves like Arizona canyons to the west. When late summer rains come, muddy water snakes through arroyos; there is no permanent river — although usually one need dig only a few feet into the dry riverbed to find wet sand. The climate is hostile even by the region's extreme standards: since Chaco was established as a National Historical Park, the National Park Service has recorded a high of 106° F. and a low of -38° F. Precipitation averages 8.7 inches a year. Tree-ring and pollen studies provide no evidence that the Anasazi enjoyed a better climate while they occupied the canyon.

But this unlikely mecca had been hunted by Paleo-Indians 7,000 years ago and farmed at least since A.D. 500.

Archaic people left some corn and squash in a rock shelter about 1000 B.C., and the first sedentary people built pithouse villages by A.D. 500. Why? Possibly it had been sporadically productive, or perhaps it was considered a place of a transcendent spiritual quality.

For some reason, between A.D. 850-900, the canyon began to embrace an astounding construction boom. The Chacoans built numerous vast pueblos (13 are now open to the public), many up to five stories high with up to 800 rooms and dozens of kivas. Archaeologists call them "great houses." They were architect-designed, conforming to site plans that from the air look like the letters D and O, or a bracket. They demanded phenomenal commitments of labor. One modern architect estimated that more than one million hand-dressed sandstone blocks went into the great house of Pueblo Bonito alone. More than 20,000 trees were cut to build Chetro Ketl. In all, an estimated 215,000 logs had to be cut and lugged into the canyon, most from forests at least 25 miles away. The problem for archeology is to imagine the social, political, and religious systems that convinced thousands of Anasazi to cooperate in building and sustaining Chaco for a century and a half.

Some clues reside in the architecture of the great houses. Unlike later canyon pueblos to the north and west, these buildings do not look as though they are huddling for defense. They express power. They do not look like towns of a people who feared harassment, but they do seem secretive. Whatever rituals were being performed in the plazas and kivas, the Pueblo's high, encircling walls would have kept outsiders' eyes away. Perhaps in Anasazi culture, just as in the medieval church of Europe, the more mystery that

(ABOVE, RIGHT) A stone stairway at Hungo Pavi Ruin, Chaco Canyon, leads to an impressive system of nearly a thousand miles of wide, straight roads radiating from Chaco Canyon to other Anasazi settlements throughout the San Juan Basin of New Mexico. These roads are thought to have been used for ceremonial as well as utilitarian purposes.
JERRY JACKA

enveloped a ritual, the more power it seemed to hold.

Power may be the best explanation of another Chacoan phenomenon: the roads. From the air, when the sun is low in the sky, they can still be seen: a system of great prehistoric paths radiating like spokes from the Chaco hub, leading to outlying communities up to 60 miles away. Although not unique to Chaco, the journalistic sensation they have caused here is. On the ground these roads are shallow depressions an inch or two deep with "curbs" of piled rock or excavated sand. They are always straight with stairways carved into the sandstone cliffs and climbing over hills rather than curling around them. While road width varies, some are uniformly 30 feet wide. Why did the Anasazi, who had no draft animals and never used the wheel, build "freeways"?

Archaeologists have a spectrum of theories. One is that Chaco, as a ritual capital, required great ceremonial procession routes. But what prehistoric ceremony would have had people walking 20 abreast for two or three days, commanded the importance to assign so much labor to the building of the roads, and yet left no record in pictographs or petroglyphs? Another theory says the roads linked colonial Chacoan pueblos with their mother great houses in the canyon, and the highways' prominence on the landscape reminded the colonists of their clan's roots.

But what *was* Chaco?

Most archaeologists today believe it was a ceremonial capital, probably maintained by a small resident population that was joined periodically by waves of people congregating for elaborate religious rituals. This theory explains several Chacoan mysteries.

One is that while the canyon's housing could have accommodated perhaps 4,000 people, its natural resources probably couldn't have supported nearly that many. Some architects think the great houses were over-engineered so a small core of permanent caretakers would have been able to maintain them. Burials in the canyon also are perplexingly scarce. Although massive post-A.D. 950 alluvial deposits 100 to 150 feet deep have effectively blocked the work of searchers, if Pueblo Bonito had been continually occupied for 150 years, it alone should have yielded some 5,000 burials. Excavations so far have discovered only about 300 burials in the entire canyon.

Archaeologist David R. Wilcox of the Museum of Northern Arizona in Flagstaff has devised a more controversial and sinister theory. Although outside the mainstream of archaeological thought, he believes Chaco was more than a ritual center; it was a city-state, ruling the New Mexico Anasazi through the threat or actual use of force. In his scenario, the roads served as reminders of Chaco's authority. If Wilcox is right, it suggests a rather unpeaceful region with rival centers of power.

Some pieces of the Chaco puzzle do fall together in his scenario. Chaco Canyon could have supported 4,000

A mosaic of turquoise overlays a bone hairpin.
JERRY JACKA

Hundreds of hand-drilled turquoise stones were strung together to make up this necklace and pendant.
GEORGE H.H. HUEY

Turquoise was the favored semi-precious stone throughout the prehistoric world and the Anasazi used it in their jewelry and art objects.

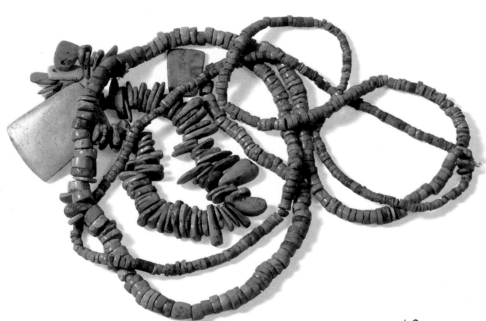

permanent residents if the Chacoans extracted tribute from their neighbors in the form of agricultural products. The phenomenal labor needed to build the great houses could have been forced. Chaco also enjoyed other forms of wealth: archaeologists have uncovered more than 60,000 pieces of turquoise shaped into beads, pendants, mosaics, and inlays. Placed into perspective, however, this would be modest compared to what has been removed from sites in Arizona's White Mountains.

Finally, Wilcox observes, around A.D. 1100 new great houses began appearing to the north, coinciding with another building boom in the canyon, circa 1075-1115 — and some were built in masonry styles foreign to the Chacoans. Wilcox thinks these were rival city-states "organized to resist further expansion of the Chacoan juggernaut."

Nature alone, however, provided resistance enough. A severe drought parched northwestern New Mexico beginning in A.D. 1130, and it persisted for half a century. This coincides precisely with the abandonment of Chaco Canyon. The last tree used in construction at Chaco was chopped in 1132, and most of the population was scattering by 1170.

If in fact it were a center of Anasazi power, Chaco collapsed for the same reason other cultures usually do: hubris. The culture challenged natural conditions with unnatural ambitions, as too many people tried to wrest a living out of a reluctant land.

Archaeologists are unsure where the Chacoan refugees went. Many may have settled in other great houses around the outlying Chaco basin. The Rio Grande Valley of New Mexico would have been another alternative, attractive because of its great river. They probably did not migrate north and west because, as Chaco faded, canyon pueblos in the other Anasazi cultural spheres of Mesa Verde and Kayenta were already burdened with growing populations and the Chacoans would have been unwelcome. When resources are stretched thin, people of different ethnic persuasions tend not to be entertained as neighbors. There may have been a powerful unifying force in the form of a new religion, however, which we will consider in Chapter 6 (see page 151).

Twilight came to most of the old Anasazi world in the late 1200s. Another great drought, this one stretching from 1276 to 1299, followed by an interval of summers with heavy rains that caused severe erosion, and then a long period of short growing seasons forced the people to abandon the northern canyons of the Colorado Plateau. Mesa Verde, Tsegi Canyon, Canyon de Chelly — all these centers of Anasazi culture were deserted during the long years of little rain.

The Anasazi didn't vanish, as is popularly believed. They became the Pueblo tribes of Arizona and New Mexico today. The Hopi mesas, though arid, had reliable springs that survived the drought. People of Acoma and Zuni moved to lower locations, but did not leave their lands. The Rio Grande was an artery that could support life even when the rains failed. Archaeologists have found that the dramatic population decline in the older Anasazi lands corresponded closely with the rise of new pueblos elsewhere.

The Hopi in particular revere their ancestors, as well they should: the roots of the complex Hopi religion and world view were formed in Anasazi times. The Hopi find it odd that outsiders keep discussing the "disappearance" of the Anasazi. In a Colorado seminar on the subject in 1990, Leigh Jenkins, the tribe's cultural preservation officer, neatly disarmed the whole issue. "If you hang around until Thursday, you'll probably find the answers to the questions being posed here because around 6 o'clock, the Anasazi will go home to Hopiland," he said. "And this Anasazi will even tell you what will take him there: a 1986 Chevy Celebrity."

(LEFT) A frog fetish made from jet (a very hard coal), with turquoise inlay.
GEORGE H.H. HUEY

Visiting the Anasazi World

Navajo National Monument

Arizona's best-preserved and most extravagant Anasazi ruins can be seen in side canyons of Tsegi Canyon, protected by national monument status and the physical effort demanded of visitors wanting to see them close up. These ruins, especially Keet Seel, are well worth the trouble.

The deep canyon alcove that shelters Keet Seel was occupied as early as A.D. 950, but the 155-room pueblo was built between 1250 and 1275. There are hints in the architecture that it was the work of people from several places and several traditions. There are remains of some unusual wattle-and-daub walls (vertical sticks chinked with clay mortar) and a unique kiva annex with a flagstone floor. The people of Keet Seel were restless. Rooms were frequently remodeled, suggesting a rapidly changing population.

Betatakin, eight miles away in a side canyon near the park entrance, is slightly smaller with an estimated 135 rooms. Archaeologists have charted its construction through dendrochronology of its roof timbers and found that trees were cut and stockpiled in A.D. 1269 and 1272, then used in a flurry of building in 1275. Apparently a cohesive group of people was expected years in advance, then quickly accommodated upon arrival. The last tree used was cut in 1286. Curiously, by 1300 Betatakin was abandoned to the spirits.

A visit to Keet Seel, "Broken Pottery" in Navajo, and Betatakin, "Ledge House," can each consume a full day.

There is no road to Keet Seel; visitors must either hike or join an eight-hour horseback excursion escorted by a Navajo wrangler. Hikers may camp overnight below the ruin. Either way the round-trip is 16 miles, and the floor of Tsegi Canyon is a morass of damp red

A visit to Betatakin Ruin at Navajo National Monument requires a moderately strenuous five-mile round-trip hike. A restricted number of visitors is allowed each day on a first-come first-served basis.
JERRY JACKA

50

(LEFT) The sloping floor of the huge alcove that shelters Betatakin provided challenges for the builders. They dug a footing groove in the sandstone, constructed a retaining wall, and filled it to allow for a level walkway at the edge of the village.
GEORGE H.H. HUEY

(FOLLOWING PANEL) It's a 16-mile round-trip hike or horseback ride to Keet Seel, also part of Navajo National Monument. The 7,000-foot elevation and sandy canyon bottom add to the effort required. But the trip is worth it, and the 20 visitors allowed at the ruin each day must make reservations at least a month in advance.
LARRY ULRICH

sand. Explorers who have tried both say the horseback ride is less exhausting. Betatakin is a five-mile round-trip hike led by a park ranger; it takes five to six hours including time in the ruins.

The number of visitors to both ruins are strictly limited. Make reservations for Keet Seel one to two months in advance. No reservations for Betatakin are needed, but line up early on the day of the tour. Keet Seel is open only Memorial Day to Labor Day; Betatakin from May through September.

Navajo National Monument, HC-71 Box 3, Tonalea, AZ 86044-9704.

Canyon De Chelly
National Monument

Modern Navajos know Canyon de Chelly as the home of Yeibichai, the Talking God, and the place from which Changing Woman departed this world to join her lover, the sun. Tourists know it as Arizona's connoisseur canyon, a 27-mile-long gash in the earth that looks not at all like the Grand Canyon but rivals it in beauty.

The Anasazi lived in Canyon de Chelly and its tributaries from near the time of Christ to A.D. 1300. The Navajos have claimed the canyon since the mid-1700s, holding it despite a massacre at the hands of Spanish soldiers in 1805.

Some 20 Navajo families still live in the canyon today, herding their sheep across the fertile canyon floor.

There are about 400 ruins in Canyon de Chelly and its main fork, Canyon del Muerto (where the Spanish massacre occurred). Visitors are allowed to approach only one, White House Ruin, without a Navajo escort. This is, however, one of the monument's most spectacular ruins. Two pueblos, one on the canyon floor and another poised in an alcove 30 feet above, are framed by colorful cottonwood and Russian olive trees (the latter an introduced species). The north canyon wall soars 400 feet over the delicate-looking upper ruin, forming a metaphor for both the fragility and determination of humankind in this land of awesome form and force. The lower ruin was occupied from A.D. 1070 to 1276. The upper ruin has not been dated.

Even at an elevation of 5,400 feet, the hike to White House Ruin is an easy 2.5-mile round-trip. Hikers have to wade the wash, which usually is no more than a foot deep. Plan to be out before dark; even though well-maintained, the trail is a 400-foot ascent and can be hazardous at night.

Navajo guides offer thorough tours of Canyon de Chelly and Canyon del Muerto on foot, horseback, or six-wheel-drive vehicles. These tours visit other ruins, Anasazi and Navajo rock-art sites, and Spider Rock, an 800-foot spire erupting from the canyon floor. The monument is open year-round.

Canyon de Chelly National Monument, P.O. Box 588, Chinle, AZ 86503.

Canyon de Chelly's spectacular scenery, ancient Anasazi cliff dwellings hidden in sandstone alcoves, and the fascinating Navajo Indians who live there today make it a required stop for anyone visiting the Southwest.
(ABOVE) Spider Rock rises more than 800 feet from the canyon floor. RANDY PRENTICE
(FACING PAGE) Exploration of White House Ruin requires a moderate hike into Canyon de Chelly. BOB AND SUZANNE CLEMENZ
(FOLLOWING PANEL) Mummy Cave Ruin in Canyon del Muerto, part of Canyon de Chelly, is named for two well-preserved burials found at the site. Portions of the ruin have been so skillfully restored that most visitors cannot tell original Anasazi construction from Park Service restorations from the early 1900s. Some of the canyon's earliest ruins are found in the cave to the left, and the most recent are to the right. RUSS FINLEY

PETRIFIED FOREST
NATIONAL PARK

The region east of Holbrook, Arizona, famous mainly for its Triassic forests preserved as logs of crystalline stone and parched Painted Desert scenery, has an annual rainfall averaging 8.6 inches. And once, for about a century, it had a substantial population of Anasazi farmers.

The Puerco River, which is usually dry, bisects the park and may have been a reliable stream in Anasazi times. A few nearby springs still bubbled water into the 20th century. The Petrified Forest Anasazi planted their crops on the mesa tops in dunes underlain by shale, the layers of which blocked seepage, and thereby retained water. But in policing their fields of weeds, the Anasazi stripped off the tough natural vegetation, inviting wind erosion. By trying to manage their environment, the prehistoric farmers may also have created more of their own desert.

Not much remains of Petrified Forest's unsheltered ruins. Puerco Ruin, once about 125 rooms, now is a foot-high stubble of the original walls. It was occupied from about A.D. 1250 to 1350, suggesting that its inhabitants had found arable land here after the canyons dried out. Agate House is a reconstructed eight-room pueblo, unique because it was built with petrified wood.

The Park Service does not advertise it, but the boulders on the south and east sides of the Puerco Ruin mesa exhibit one of the most concentrated petroglyph collections in the region. The Anasazi "Nureyev" is immortalized here, an exuberant dancer frozen in stone. Also hidden among the boulders is a summer solstice marker that continues to acknowledge silently the sun's seasonal migration early in the morning every June 21.

Petrified Forest National Park, P.O. Box 2217, Petrified Forest, AZ 86028.

(ABOVE, LEFT) Puerco Ruin, Petrified Forest National Park. Three kivas and 33 of the 125 rooms have been excavated at this rectangular mesa-top pueblo above the Puerco River. A number of artifacts chipped from petrified wood indicate tool making was a major activity there. TOM TILL

(ABOVE, RIGHT) An impressive array of petroglyphs such as this "dancer" have been scratched into the rocks to the south and east of Puerco Ruin. LAWRENCE W. CHEEK

HOMOLOVI
RUINS STATE PARK

Homolovi, near Winslow, Arizona, is another very late Anasazi settlement, occupied intermittently between A.D. 1250 and 1400. Archaeologists suspect it was selected because of the great drought. Visit in spring or late summer and see why: the broad alluvial floodplain of the Little Colorado River, just to the west, will indeed be flooded. In wet years the flooding wiped out farmlands in its path, but in relatively dry years there might have been just enough water to be beneficial. This was the experience, at least, of the Mormon farmers who followed the Anasazi here.

Visitors see the remains of two large pueblos, along with a collection of clan petroglyphs about 200 yards west of the Homolovi II ruin. The site was

dedicated as a state park in 1986. Unfortunately that was long after pothunters had done massive damage.

Homolovi Ruins State Park, HC-63, Box 5, Winslow, AZ 86047.

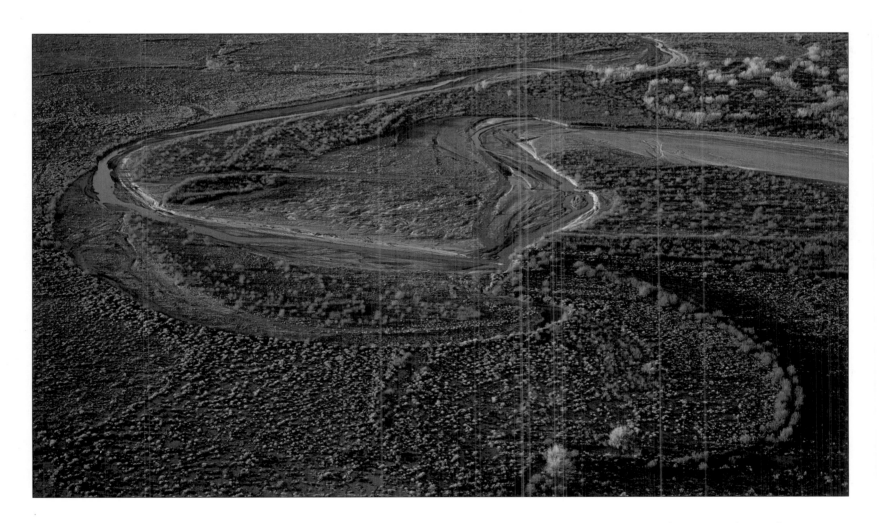

(ABOVE) The meandering Little Colorado River near Homolovi Ruins State Park. In addition to corn, beans, and squash, the Homolovi Anasazi farmed cotton on the floodplain of the Little Colorado below their villages. MICHAEL COLLIER

(TOP) A pronghorn antelope petroglyph near Homolovi Ruins. When the first Europeans arrived on the high plateau of northeastern Arizona, herds of these animals roamed the desert grasslands. GEORGE H.H. HUEY

GRAND CANYON NATIONAL PARK

At one time or another, the Anasazi occupied some 2,000 sites in and around the Grand Canyon. They might have been drawn to it for at least one of the same reasons we are today: its awesome grandeur. Tusayan, on the Grand Canyon's South Rim, is the most accessible ruin; the paved park road, State Route 64, passes close by.

Judging from the rubble, archaeologists suspect Tusayan was two stories high and had 15 rooms. Only two generations of Anasazi lived here from A.D. 1185 to 1225. Once a small settlement such as this burned up the supply of nearby firewood, it was easier for the inhabitants to go elsewhere than to haul wood from an ever-widening radius.

Limestone walls two feet high are all that remain of Tusayan. Limestone is much harder than sandstone, so these rocks were not artfully shaped into building blocks as in pueblos to the east. The ruin lies four miles west of the Desert View park entrance.

Grand Canyon National Park, Grand Canyon, AZ 86023.

(ABOVE) Among the least accessible and most fascinating of the more than 2,000 Anasazi ruins at the Grand Canyon, the Nankoweep granaries peer down upon the Colorado River with empty eyes.
JERRY JACKA

(RIGHT) Near the Desert View entrance to Grand Canyon National Park, Tusayan Ruins and museum explain the Anasazi who lived on the rim of this scenic wonder.
JAMES TALLON

HOVENWEEP
NATIONAL MONUMENT

Hovenweep, a Ute word meaning "deserted valley," is almost as enigmatic as Chaco Canyon. It is located in southeastern Utah, tight against the borders of Arizona and Colorado. There are six major groups of ruins in the monument, but five are difficult to reach. Square Tower Ruin is the best preserved, most impressive, and most accessible. Throughout the monument, buildings perch on the brows of canyons, and the only apparent entrances are from the canyon side. Towers burst from the canyon rims and floor, and some are even constructed precariously atop rock formations, so the architecture seemingly becomes an extension of the rock itself.

A number of theories struggle to explain Hovenweep's unique buildings. Defense is one: towers may have been useful for signaling and thwarting surprise invaders. But many of Hovenweep's high rises are on sites that have little or no use in reconnaissance. Astronomy? At the ruin fancifully named Hovenweep Castle, sunlight at the winter solstice slips through a port to illuminate an interior lintel; at summer solstice the same phenomenon occurs on a different alignment. Three other solar observatories are suspected in nearby towers.

In prehistoric times, terraces in draws leading to the canyon probably captured water and soil for floodwater irrigation of crops. Hovenweep was doubtless serviced by springs, but in general the region could best be described as marginal for subsistence living and the buildings were occupied only from A.D. 1150 to 1250. In modern times the ranger station has recorded a high of 105° F., a low of -24° F., and average annual precipitation of 11.7 inches.

Hovenweep National Monument is open all year, but roads into the monument are unpaved and may be treacherous in rain or snow.

Hovenweep National Monument, McElmo Route, Cortez, CO 81321.

Hovenweep Castle seemingly grows from the sandstone at the edge of Square Tower Canyon, Hovenweep National Monument, Utah. The National Park Service has stabilized a number of the high-walled circular and D-shaped towers of Hovenweep.
TOM DANIELSEN

MESA VERDE NATIONAL PARK

Benjamin Wetherill, one of the first modern Americans to explore Mesa Verde, wrote, "It was so much like treading 'holy ground' to go into the peaceful-looking homes of a vanished people." With 800,000 park visitors every year, the homes may no longer appear peaceful, but one's sense of awe remains as profound as Wetherill's. Situated between Cortez and Durango in Colorado, these are some of the most beautiful, dramatic, scalp-tingling prehistoric ruins in North America.

Mesa Verde ("Green Table" in Spanish) is a forested, canyon-gouged flat-topped mountain that, curiously, enjoys a milder climate than the valley 2,500 feet below. Cold air spilling downslope from the mesa slides under the valley's warmer air, pushing it up toward the higher elevations. As a result, the mesa's growing season stretches 20 days longer than the valley's. The Anasazi took advantage of this and began farming on the mountain around A.D. 600.

The great canyon pueblos were built between A.D. 1200 and 1276, after which Mesa Verdeans migrated to the Rio Grande Valley. Spruce Tree House and Cliff Palace are the two largest and most spectacular ruins, and visitors are permitted inside. (Spruce Tree also is one of the few Anasazi ruins with a wheelchair-accessible trail.) Cliff Palace, the largest cliff dwelling in North America, has 217 rooms, 23 kivas, and could have accommodated a population of 200 to 250. It is a miniature town, not a palace. No modern city exudes such a breathless architectural commotion, yet Cliff Palace grows so gracefully from its site that it seems like an extension of Nature.

Budgeting a full day to see Mesa Verde is not nearly enough. There are numerous ruins, a worthwhile 2.8-mile round-trip hike to Pictograph Point, and the most complete museum in any of the Anasazi parks or monuments. The visitors center has a handout with useful tips on photographing the ruins. The park has a cafeteria, and a lodge is open May through October. Mesa Verde is open all year, but from December through February only Spruce Tree House may be toured.

Mesa Verde National Park, P.O. Box 8, Mesa Verde, CO 81330.

(LEFT)
A detail of Spruce Tree House with a ladder protruding from an entrance to a kiva.
TOM DANIELSEN

(ABOVE) An overview of Spruce Tree House, named for the ancient spruces growing near the ruin. The cliff dwelling features prominently in a Hopi Indian legend recounted in Frank Waters' *Book of the Hopi*, where the badger clan quarreled with other clans in their village and caused a drought and starvation. The clan elder said it was time to continue their migration, but he was too old to make the trip. He told the others to go, but to return in four years and look for a sign from him. When the clan came back, they found the pueblo's once-dry spring again flowing and beside it, a young spruce tree was growing.
JERRY JACKA

(FOLLOWING PANEL) Long House Ruin, Mesa Verde. TOM TILL

UTE MOUNTAIN TRIBAL PARK

This 195-square-mile park on the Ute Mountain Reservation is the best-kept archaeological secret in Colorado. Although it abuts Mesa Verde National Park, only 2,500 visitors a year have noticed it. One explores these ruins almost alone.

All-day tours visit several petroglyph sites and four canyon pueblos: Tree House, Lion House, Morris 5 (named for Earl Morris, an early Southwestern archaeologist), and the aptly named Eagle's Nest. Touring all four requires a three-mile mountainside hike. It is not dangerous, but those with acrophobia may find it unsettling.

Tribal guides must accompany all visitors, and reservations are required. Bring drinking water, lunch, and hiking shoes. Tours begin at the park visitors center near the junction of U.S. routes 160 and 666, 20 miles south of Cortez. Ruins tours are suspended during winter.

Ute Mountain Tribal Park, General Delivery, Towaoc, CO 81334.

CHACO CULTURE NATIONAL HISTORICAL PARK

The ruins of Chaco Canyon are immense, but one of the unadvertised pleasures lies in examining its masonry intimately, inch by inch. It is a way of coming to know the Anasazi as individual people.

Archaeologists have identified five distinctive masonry styles in the 13 Chacoan great houses. Amateur observers can look at the walls and also discern something of the personalities of the builders. One wall of a room may be built in the banded Bonito style, where a course of thick sandstone blocks will be separated by three or four thin slabs 1/4 to 1/2 inch thick, while another wall will comprise exactly fitted stones of nearly the same size. Some ancient masons flattened the exterior sides of the blocks, others let jagged edges protrude.

(LEFT) The aptly named Eagle's Nest Ruin is the most spectacular of four Anasazi ruins on guided tours of Ute Mountain Tribal Park. Timbers protruding from the front of the ruin probably supported a catwalk that hung out over the abyss.
LAWRENCE W. CHEEK

Some were meticulous, some were sloppy.

The most finely dressed masonry is in the perimeter walls, which suggests that the Chacoans were most concerned about their cities' outward appearance. The great houses expressed communal power, not individual luxury.

Even a short visit to Chaco demands half a day and should include the two largest great houses of Pueblo Bonito and neighboring Chetro Ketl and the restored great kiva of Casa Rinconada across the wash. (Archaeologist Stephen Lekson wittily calls this area "downtown Chaco.") A day-long visit should incorporate the pueblos of Una Vida, Hungo Pavi. Kin Kletso, Pueblo del Arroyo, and a hike up the trail behind Kin Kletso to the rim for an eagle's-eye view of Kin Kletso, Pueblo Bonito, and Chetro Ketl. The trail is only slightly strenuous, but hikers should carry water in any season.

When you go be sure your gas tank is full and pack a lunch. Chaco is about 75 miles south of Aztec, 30 miles of which are on a dirt road; or about 90 miles northwest of Grants, including 20 miles of dirt road. There is no food, gas, or lodging, but the Park Service does maintain a campground a mile from the visitors center. Beware of these roads in inclement weather.

The park is open daily from a half-hour before sunrise to a half-hour after sunset.

Chaco Culture National Historical Park, Star Route 4, Box 6500, Bloomfield, NM 87413.

(ABOVE, LEFT) Pueblo Bonito Ruin at Chaco Canyon was first excavated in 1896 and yielded a treasure trove of cultural artifacts which were sent to the American Museum of Natural History.
(ABOVE) A short hike provides a strikingly different perspective of Wiji i Ruin, one of the smaller sites at Chaco Canyon.
BOTH BY LARRY ULRICH

AZTEC RUINS NATIONAL MONUMENT

The 500-room great house that modern Americans fancifully call Aztec Pueblo was built between A.D. 1106 and 1124, about 50 crow-flight miles north of "downtown Chaco." Aztec followed on the heels of the great Chaco building boom, and standard archaeological thinking is that this pueblo was a regional capital or outpost, a short-lived attempt to extend the Chacoan political system.

Despite the Animas River splashing by just a short walk away, the Chacoans drifted out of the area about A.D. 1150-1170. The signature of pottery styles shows that some early refugees from Mesa Verde, 40 miles to the northwest, then claimed Aztec beginning around 1225. Shortly before 1300, it was abandoned again.

Archaeologist Earl Morris reconstructed Aztec's ruined great kiva in 1934. As the only reroofed prehistoric great kiva in the Southwest, it offers a hint of a kiva's ambience in Anasazi times. Easy to reach on paved roads, at the edge of the community by the same name, Aztec is open year-around.

Aztec Ruins National Monument, P.O. Box 640, Aztec, NM 87410.

EL MORRO NATIONAL MONUMENT

El Morro ("The Bluff"), a sandstone monolith bursting 200 feet out of the high Colorado Plateau, has attracted both permanent residents and transient graffiti artists across the last millennium.

A natural pool at the base of the mesa collects late summer rain and stores it throughout the year; when full it holds about 200,000 gallons. This was an obvious attraction for the prehistoric people who built the pueblo of Atsinna on the mesa top around A.D. 1275. Both round and square kivas are still visible, suggesting that people from both Anasazi and

Mogollon lands, fleeing tribulations, made a deal at El Morro to live peaceably together. This large pueblo, numbering approximately 875 rooms, was abandoned about 1350.

Not much remains of Atsinna, but visitors following the trail up to the ruin may study the very readable historic inscriptions of Spanish and American pioneers who stopped by for a drink, beginning with Juan de Oñate, the first governor of New Mexico, in 1605. For perspective, this was 15 years before the Pilgrims docked at Plymouth Rock. Open year-round.

El Morro National Monument, Route 2, Box 43, Ramah, NM 87321.

(ABOVE, RIGHT) Atsinna Ruin, El Morro National Monument, had more than 1,000 rooms in its heyday. The 200,000 gallon natural water tank attracted countless prehistoric people. Among them were the Zuni Indians who today live 40 miles to the west. GEORGE H.H. HUEY
(ABOVE) An aerial view of Aztec National Monument with its reconstructed great Kiva.
RUSS FINLEY

BANDELIER
NATIONAL MONUMENT

Bandelier, about 90 minutes from Santa Fe, New Mexico, nearly forged a link between prehistoric Anasazi and historic Pueblo times. The big villages here were occupied from about A.D. 1175 to 1550. Coronado's expedition in 1540 might have passed within a few miles, but the Spaniards overlooked them. There is no mention of these pueblos in the chronicles of Coronado's *entrada*.

Bandelier National Monument, established in 1916, is named for Adolph F. A. Bandelier, a Swiss-American geologist who, like so many self-trained pioneer archaeologists, surrendered another career to spend the rest of his life struggling to understand Southwestern prehistory. Bandelier's obsession also yielded an ethnohistorical novel, *The Delight Makers*, which is set in the monument's Frijoles Canyon. More than 70 miles of maintained trails lace through the craggy natural scenery and ruins at Bandelier. Visitors in good physical condition should not miss Ceremonial Cave, a canyon-wall kiva demanding a 140-foot climb up a series of ladders.

Bandelier National Monument, HCR 1, Box 1, Suite 15, Los Alamos, NM 87544-9701.

(ABOVE) An impressive array of prehistoric rock art decorates Painted Cave,
Bandelier National Monument. RUSS FINLEY
(FOLLOWING PANEL) The reward for an arduous climb, the kiva at Ceremonial Cave,
in the forested Frijole Canyon, Bandelier National Monument. LAURENCE PARENT

PETROGLYPH NATIONAL MONUMENT

Established by Congress in 1990, this National Monument northwest of Albuquerque protects the more than 15,000 petroglyphs pecked on the rocks of the 17-mile-long lava escarpment here. Contemporary Pueblo Indians consider the entire monument a sacred landscape, an area that commands respect and care.

Although some petroglyphs could be as much as 2,000 to 3,000 years old, most were created after A.D. 1300. In addition to the petroglyphs, more than 100 archaeological sites tell the 12,000-year-long story of human habitation in the area. There seems to be an endless variety of images — animals, stick figures, masks, spirals, and abstract shapes. Enjoy the images and take photographs of them, but please do not touch, make tracings, or otherwise disturb the rocks. This is a fragile, nonrenewable cultural resource.

Not all of the monument is open to the public at this time. However, there are three self-guided trails.

Petroglyph National Monument, National Park Service, 4735 Unser Blvd., NW, Albuquerque, NM 87120.

CORONADO STATE MONUMENT

Archaeological investigations at Kuaua (Tiwa for "Evergreen") were conducted from 1934 to 1939. They yielded one of the most important discoveries in the history of Pueblo studies, a nearly intact set of multicolored kiva murals. These murals, which had been painted on layers of plaster, were transported to the University of New Mexico where they were carefully removed and attached to Masonite. They are now on display in the monument's museum building.

The importance of the development of the kachina cult in Pueblo society can not be overstated. The murals discovered here, depicting animals and human forms, are some of the finest examples of prehistoric kiva art to be found anywhere. The centerpiece of this state monument is the old Kuaua village, first settled about A.D. 1300, and its magnificently restored kiva. Descending the ladder into the kiva's dimly lit interior gives one the feeling of going back in time.

Located on the west bank of the Rio Grande approximately 15 miles north of Albuquerque, just outside Bernalillo, the monument is adjacent to Coronado State Park.

For additional information, contact the Museum of New Mexico, P.O. Box 2087, Santa Fe, NM 87503.

(ABOVE, LEFT) Thousands of petroglyphs have been pecked into the boulder-strewn cliffs above the Rio Grande River at Petroglyph National Monument near Albuquerque, New Mexico.
MARK NOHL

(ABOVE, RIGHT) Zuni interpretation of the Kuaua Ruin kiva murals, according to archaeologist Bertha Dutton's book *Sun Father's Way*, says this is a portion of the universe.
JERRY JACKA

74

CHAPTER TWO

SINAGUA

...TRADERS IN THE LAND OF LITTLE WATER

It must have been an extravagant funeral. We cannot know what words or prayers or songs were offered to speed the dead man's spiritual voyage into the next world, but we know exactly what was going with him: a lavish treasury of more than 600 ceramic vessels, baskets, tools, mosaic-encrusted jewelry, shell pendants, arrowheads, and a dozen ceremonial wooden wands. The stunningly beautiful wands were carved and painted like deer hooves, antelope hooves, and human hands; and there were three of each type. Because of these, archaeologists named the obviously important man buried with them "the Magician."

Archaeologists stumbled onto the Magician's grave in 1941 while excavating Ridge Ruin about 15 miles east of Flagstaff. It was a stunning discovery because it confirmed an advanced level of social organization by the 12th century and clearly demonstrated that the Magician's people had complex religious societies. When Hopi elders examined the wands, the remarkable endurance of pueblo tradition also became apparent. The modern Hopis linked the Magician with their Motswimi, or warrior society, and knew exactly what the Magician would have done with the wands: he would have conducted a ceremony for the strengthening of a particular individual or group. The Hopis said that this ritual had remained in their tribal repertoire until the 19th century.

The Magician was a member of the amorphous Sinagua culture that farmed the land from modern Flagstaff north and east to the Little Colorado River and the Verde River Valley 40 miles to the south. "Sinagua" is Spanish for "Without Water," which would have described the situation at least of the Sinagua in the area of present-day Wupatki National Monument. The 12,643-foot San Francisco Peaks steal most of the moisture from the eastbound storms rumbling across the Colorado Plateau; Wupatki today averages 8.5 inches of precipitation a year. In other areas the Sinaguans enjoyed a somewhat wetter climate, however.

Archaeologists are stumped by the Sinagua. Harold S. Colton concluded in the 1940s that they were a branch of the Mogollon culture. Harold S. Gladwin thought they looked like Anasazi. Modern Sinagua specialist Christian E. Downum, an archaeologist at Northern Arizona University, considers them a mosaic of people with too many variations in architecture, artifacts, and burial practices to form a neat and coherent culture.

The Sinagua are recognized in the archaeological record later than Anasazi, Hohokam, or Mogollon, with their undecorated brownware pottery appearing around the San Francisco Peaks about A.D. 600. From 600 to 1100 they

(LEFT) Turquoise mosaic adorns a bird-shaped shell pendant found near Montezuma Castle National Monument. GEORGE H.H. HUEY

(PAGE 75) This six-inch Sinagua stone effigy was found near Flagstaff. JERRY JACKA
(LEFT) Wukoki Ruin seems to rise from a large boulder. TOM DANIELSEN
(FOLLOWING PANEL) Lomaki Ruin, beneath the looming San Francisco Peaks, is surrounded by fields where Sinagua farmers once raised corn, beans, and squash. RICHARD WESTON

Prehistoric weavers used a variety of
tools and techniques to transform plant fibers
into useful and sometimes decorative
fabric and basketry.
(CLOCKWISE FROM ABOVE, LEFT)
Sinagua woven cotton bag found at
Montezuma Castle National Monument.
GEORGE H.H. HUEY
Fragment of cotton fabric with a woven
design probably was made using
bone needles. JERRY JACKA
Woven yucca fiber sandals.
GEORGE H.H. HUEY
Stones were used to sharpen awls and
needles like this bone awl which
probably was used as a hole punch
in basket making.
JERRY JACKA

lived in square or rectangular pithouses and stone field houses, which probably were temporary shelters for farmers tending remote fields.

A few unusually large pits, some as much as 30 feet across and five feet deep, have been found in even the earliest Sinagua settlements. These likely were community rooms for ceremonies or socializing. Like the Magician's grave, the early appearance of large pithouses hints that they had already developed a somewhat complex social culture. This, of course, only darkens the fog around their origins. Where did the complexity come from?

One good possibility: the Sinagua were avid traders and readily adopted customs and life-styles from their neighbors. Hohokam-style ball courts began to appear in Sinagua lands around A.D. 900, Anasazi-style pueblo architecture by 1100. Hohokam pithouses have even been found mingled in Sinagua sites, meaning either that wanderers were welcome to establish residence or that "foreign" traders lived temporarily among the Sinagua.

In a different respect the Sinagua were oddly unsophisticated. Unlike the Hohokam, Mogollon, and Anasazi, the Sinagua never developed painted pottery as an art. The pottery they did make is very much like the plainware of the Hohokam. With few exceptions, Sinagua ceramics are undecorated and undistinguished. They imported elegant kitchenware from their neighbors. Why

they chose not to adopt this widely practiced prehistoric art form, and what they had to trade for it, are mysteries.

In A.D. 1064 the world of the northern Sinagua erupted — literally. The volcano now called Sunset Crater spewed cinders and ash over 800 square miles of northern Arizona. A curious human commotion followed the geologic one. After briefly fleeing the growling mountain, people flocked to its shadow.

For decades, conventional archaeological wisdom held that the black blanket of volcanic ash and cinder suddenly enhanced the region's agricultural potential by draining nutrients into the soil and creating a covering "mulch" that discouraged evaporation. Word of the newly fertile farmlands flashed across prehistoric Arizona, igniting a land rush. Hohokam, Mogollon, and Anasazi people streamed into the territory, and the accommodating Sinagua welcomed them.

But archaeologists today are rethinking the scenario surrounding this prehistoric melting pot. Forest Service archaeologist Peter J. Pilles, Jr. points out that volcanic spew fertilizes soil slowly over millennia, not quickly in months or years. For proof, Pilles examined the sparse vegetation around Wupatki and the stunted ponderosa pines immediately beside 900-year-old Sunset Crater volcano today. Pondering the

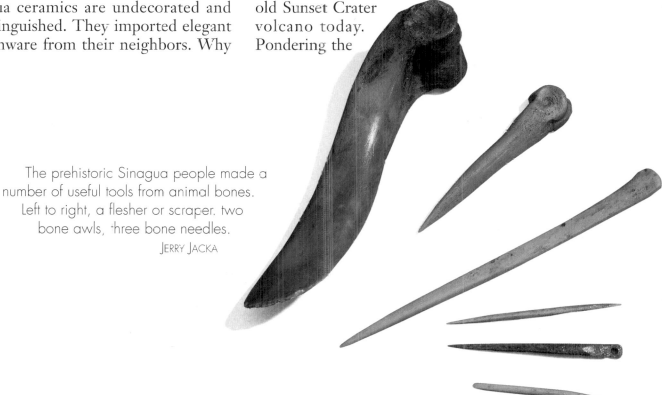

The prehistoric Sinagua people made a number of useful tools from animal bones. Left to right, a flesher or scraper, two bone awls, three bone needles.
JERRY JACKA

rainfall records in tree rings, Pilles argued that the Sinagua simply took advantage of a 100-year-long wet spell, from A.D. 1050 to 1150, by moving into what had formerly been unproductive lowlands. The surge of alien pottery and jewelry, in his view, came from the Sinaguans' penchant for trading and the fact that in a time of prosperity they had more to trade.

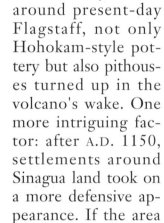

Plain Sinagua brownware pottery from Walnut Canyon. TOM BEAN

On the other hand, many post-eruption Sinagua pueblos look distinctly Anasazi. Wukoki, Crack-in-Rock Ruin, and the Citadel almost certainly are. All around present-day Flagstaff, not only Hohokam-style pottery but also pithouses turned up in the volcano's wake. One more intriguing factor: after A.D. 1150, settlements around Sinagua land took on a more defensive appearance. If the area had become multicultural through 100 years of plentiful rain, then commonsense archaeology says the onset of drought would have caused tensions among the different "nationalities" living so near each other.

Whoever they were, between A.D. 1225 and 1300 the people in the Flagstaff area drifted away, some to the Hopi

mesas, some to the Verde Valley, or elsewhere. The southern Sinagua continued to prosper in the Verde Valley for at least another century; the mystery there is why they, too, eventually disappeared. Of all the riparian environments in Arizona, the verdant Verde, which drains a forested watershed of 6,000 square miles, would be among the most likely to continue supporting complex communities no matter what happened to the climate.

This southern group further complicates the thorny questions about Sinaguan identity. Until A.D. 1000 they looked a lot like Hohokam, with red-on-buff pottery, shell jewelry, and burial by cremation. Then cultural diversity appeared to increase along with trade goods from among the northern Sinagua and Anasazi. Hohokam influence waned, then disappeared. Several possibilities exist: the southern Sinagua could have been Hohokam who gradually adopted the Puebloan ways of their northern neighbors. Or the Hohokam might have been pushed out of the valley by an unfriendly surge from the north. Or the valley might have been multicultural throughout its prehistory with the patterns of settlement naturally changing and evolving over time.

Faced with what appears to be a hopelessly tangled Sinaguan identity crisis, archaeology has all but conceded defeat. Christian E. Downum has as conclusive a last word as there is: "There were, evidently, many ways to be Sinagua."

Sandstone, volcanic stones, and clay mortar create a pleasing texture and a sturdy wall at Citadel Ruin, Wupatki National Monument. TOM BEAN

Olivella shell necklace with an argillite pendant, from Montezuma Castle. GEORGE H.H. HUEY

Wupatki Ruin with its sunken "ball court." Courts like this appear throughout the Southwest,
and archaeologists believe they were used for games that may have had religious
significance. The game may have been similar to one Spanish conquistadors
reported seeing the Mayas of Mexico playing in the 1500s.
LAURENCE PARENT

(**ABOVE**) Montezuma Well, Montezuma Castle National Monument. This
spring-fed limestone sink, 470 feet in diameter, gushes 1.5 million
gallons of water a day.
(**RIGHT**) The Sinaguans built several small dwellings around the interior of this
natural bowl and used its water for irrigation in surrounding fields.
BOTH BY GEORGE H.H. HUEY

VISITING THE SINAGUA WORLD

WALNUT CANYON
NATIONAL MONUMENT

Expert rock-climbers of our own time have tried winter descents into Walnut Canyon, a rocky, 385-foot-deep furrow in the ponderosa forest seven miles east of Flagstaff. On the canyon's south-facing rim they encountered slippery moss and on the north-facing rim, ice. Their report: "very scary" for the south-facing route, "impossible" on the north-facing rim.

What could have convinced a community of Sinagua to build some 300 dwellings in Walnut Canyon, many of them under an overhang halfway between the canyon rims and floor? Agricultural fields were above; Walnut Creek trickled seasonally below. People commuted via a system of trails, today obscured by vegetation. At an elevation of 6,600 feet the growing season was short. However lovely it looked, this canyon presented its residents with a marginal environment for survival — and because the Sinagua didn't move in until about A.D. 1125, approaching the last chapter of their history, they probably knew it.

Why settle such a difficult place? Population in Sinagua territory was expanding during this period, and the better sites were already taken. Defense may have been a selling point, even if it did require precarious climbing. Yet at the same time there was an unprotected pueblo on top of the canyon's north rim. Like so many issues in Southwestern archaeology, the solution to this riddle is not at all clear.

There is no evidence of major warfare in Walnut Canyon, but we know of at least one Sinaguan killed here by an alien arrow. Excavating a burial ground in 1966, archaeologist Norman Ritchie found part of an arrowhead lodged in the rib cage of a 30- to 35-year-old woman. The obsidian arrowhead had an elaborately carved base, unlike any others he found. It is a tantalizing hint of a prehistoric confrontation, but by itself, no proof that there was more than one stray invader.

Walnut Canyon became a national monument in 1915, too late to save it from devastating vandalism. Pothunters not only snatched invaluable artifacts, but even dynamited some prehistoric walls, says the Park Service, "to let in more light." A few dwellings have been stabilized so they appear in virtually original form, and visitors may stoop and squeeze in through the diminutive doorways. A valuable exercise, this demonstrates how small, cold, and dark Sinagua houses could be.

Walnut Canyon National Monument, Walnut Canyon Road, Flagstaff, AZ 86004.

(ABOVE) Snow frosts the ruins along Island Trail, Walnut Canyon National Monument.
(RIGHT) The San Francisco Peaks, home of the kachina spirits of contemporary Hopi Indians, loom above cliffside ruins in Walnut Canyon.
BOTH BY TOM BEAN

WUPATKI
NATIONAL MONUMENT

The road into Wupatki is always open, and connoisseurs know to time their arrival for sunrise — when utter silence towers over the high country desert, the sense of isolation is profound, and first light paints the sandstone ruins in the colors of fire.

A T-shaped doorway at Lomaki Ruin.
FRANK ZULLO

This national monument exhibits the ruins of Sinagua architecture at its most ambitious and expressive — except that a lot of it probably was not Sinaguan. The huge 100-room pueblo (Wupatki Pueblo) behind the visitors center looks suspiciously like a Chacoan great house and was built beginning around A.D. 1120, close to the time that the Chaco exodus began. The masonry looks like Kayenta Anasazi, and the abandonment of Wupatki began around 1225, about the same time the Kayenta building boom commenced. There also is a prominent ball court, indicating that the Wupatkians, whoever they were, had plugged into the ceremonial network of the Hohokam culture far to the south.

Not much is clear about Wupatki but this: it was briefly one of the Southwest's most important prehistoric crossroads and trade centers, a regional capital nearly equivalent to Casas Grandes and Chaco Canyon.

Wupatki Pueblo is the largest ruin in the monument, but the much smaller Wukoki ruin is the most striking and most often photographed. A two-story, six-room complex that might have housed an extended family, it buds from a sandstone promontory with such organic grace that it is as if the spirits had said to the human builders, "We're tired of sculpting this rock; you finish the job." This was not an easy rock to finish sculpting, and defense was obviously not a concern. It wasn't even a good lookout — a ridge to the north offers higher ground. However, the "prow" of the rock points toward San Francisco Peaks, which modern Hopi believe to be the home of their kachina spirits. Assuming their ancestors believed likewise, that might well explain Wukoki's dramatic siting.

Wupatki National Monument, HC-33, P.O. Box 444A, Flagstaff, AZ 86001.

(LEFT) Sunrise illuminates Crack-in-Rock Ruin, Wupatki National Monument.
To protect this ruin, the Park Service requires visitors to reserve space
on one of eight guided overnight hikes annually.
DAVID H. SMITH
(ABOVE) A pronghorn antelope herds her young in this Sinagua petroglyph.
TOM BEAN

MONTEZUMA CASTLE NATIONAL MONUMENT

More than 100 years ago Charles Lummis wrote, "A castle it truly looks . . . and a much finer ruin than many that people rush abroad to see along the historic Rhine." Lummis was a newspaperman who hiked from Ohio to California in 1884, filing dispatches to the *Los Angeles Times* en route.

Lummis was romanticizing, but not quite as much as the U.S. Army scouts who had stumbled across the ruin 20 years earlier and named it "Montezuma Castle," figuring that only the great Aztec emperor could have commissioned it.

The "castle" was built not by Aztecs but by the Verde Valley Sinagua. There were about 65 rooms in the craggy limestone cliff and another pueblo at the cliff's base.

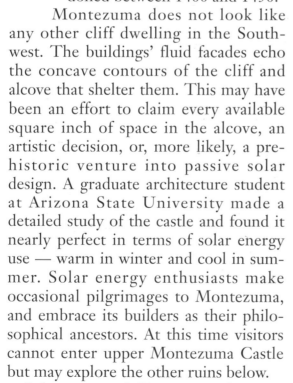

Sinagua woven basket found at Montezuma Castle.
GEORGE H.H. HUEY

The sycamore logs used in construction do not supply reliable tree-ring dates, so archaeologists can only guess at Montezuma's age by reading pottery types. It was built sometime between A.D. 1100 and 1350, and abandoned between 1400 and 1450.

Montezuma does not look like any other cliff dwelling in the Southwest. The buildings' fluid facades echo the concave contours of the cliff and alcove that shelter them. This may have been an effort to claim every available square inch of space in the alcove, an artistic decision, or, more likely, a prehistoric venture into passive solar design. A graduate architecture student at Arizona State University made a detailed study of the castle and found it nearly perfect in terms of solar energy use — warm in winter and cool in summer. Solar energy enthusiasts make occasional pilgrimages to Montezuma, and embrace its builders as their philosophical ancestors. At this time visitors cannot enter upper Montezuma Castle but may explore the other ruins below.

Other unusual Sinagua settlements line Montezuma Well, a limestone water bowl 400 feet across and 65 feet deep, 11 miles northeast of Montezuma Castle. Tiny cliff dwellings squeeze into fissures in the bowl's upper rim and

base. In prehistoric times the small human community that lived here used Hohokam irrigation technology to water their fields nearby. Some of those ditches are still being used today.

Montezuma Castle National Monument, P.O. Box 219, Camp Verde, AZ 86332.

(ABOVE) Massive sycamore trees frame a wintry view of Montezuma Castle.
The cliff dwelling, which rises to five stories, was built of small limestone blocks
and roofed with sycamore logs, poles, sticks, grass, and mud.
DAVID MUENCH
(FOLLOWING PANEL) The low hilltop pueblo of Tuzigoot National Monument presents
a completely different style of Sinagua architecture.
JERRY JACKA

TUZIGOOT
NATIONAL MONUMENT

In 1932 Frank Lloyd Wright articulated his philosophy about buildings and their sites: "No house should ever be on any hill . . . it should be of the hill, belonging to it, so hill and house could live together each the happier for the other."

Wright's own century mostly ignored his wisdom, but 800 years before he gave it, the Verde Valley Sinagua had constructed a perfect illustration of the principle. Tuzigoot pueblo crowns a 100-foot-high ridge overlooking the Verde River so gracefully and inevitably that the hill would seem unfinished without it. By modern standards it could not have been a comfortable place to live, but it gave no offense to the landscape it occupied. A visit to Tuzigoot is a lesson in architectural aesthetics as well as in archaeology.

This was almost surely circumstantial. The builders of Tuzigoot were not trying to express anything, as were their Anasazi contemporaries at Chaco Canyon. They were simply limited by resources and technology from doing any damage. They couldn't gouge the hill with bulldozers; they had no choice but to follow its contours. Why they used the hill is open to speculation. The site was floodproof, and it would have been slightly warmer than the valley floor because of the cold-sink effect (cool air sliding down and under the valley's warm air lifts the latter). But it also is a natural perch for wary people — it provides commanding views of the valley in every direction — and apparently it became more defensive over time: at some point ground-floor doorways were sealed, leaving only rooftop entrances. By the time Tuzigoot was abandoned, just one outside doorway still existed.

Tuzigoot (an Apache word for "Crooked Water," referring to nearby Pecks Lake) was begun in A.D. 1076 and abandoned around 1425.

Tuzigoot National Monument, P.O. Box 68, Clarkdale, AZ 86324.

At its peak Tuzigoot probably housed more than 200 people who farmed the rich bottomlands along the Verde River.
JERRY JACKA

CHAPTER THREE

MOGOLLON

...THE FIRST MOUNTAIN FARMERS

As a prehistoric people, the Mogollon did not really arrive until A.D. 1936. Until this late date, the pithouse and pueblo people of the highlands straddling Arizona, New Mexico, and the bordering Mexican state of Chihuahua were vaguely believed to be an alloy of Anasazi and Hohokam. In 1936, after three years of painstaking excavations beside New Mexico's San Francisco and Mimbres rivers, archaeologist Emil Haury declared the Mogollon to be a distinct people who had been making pottery before anyone else in the region. Haury's bomb shattered the tidy world of Southwestern prehistory, although the Mogollon were not fully accepted until the 1960s.

Even today the Mogollon remains a murky, difficult-to-define culture. The great pueblo of Paquimé (also called Casas Grandes) in Chihuahua, Mexico, is popularly attributed to a group of unusually ambitious Mogollon, but it actually was a Mesoamerican trading center grafted onto Mogollon roots. Meanwhile, in northern Arizona and New Mexico, the Mogollon fused with the Anasazi so thoroughly that archaeologists still dispute which was which.

A chameleon culture? Apparently, and one destined to furrow the brows of many generations of archaeologists. But the achievements ascribed to the Mogollon are as impressive as the people are baffling: Paquimé, with its carefully engineered municipal water and sewer systems; Mimbres ceramics, the most elaborately and mysteriously decorated pots ever produced in prehistoric North America; and the recently discovered crypts of Casa Malpais, the only known Indian burials of this type in the country.

Like the Anasazi, the Mogollon slowly evolved from Archaic hunter-gatherers into farmers and village-dwellers. The earliest Mogollon-area potsherds were associated with material radiocarbon-dated about A.D. 1, and pithouse villages showed up by A.D. 200. As with the Anasazi, material progress in these embryonic centuries was slow.

In the Casas Grandes Valley of Chihuahua, Mexico, about 200 miles southwest of El Paso, Texas, Mogollon people had been living in flimsy pithouses since A.D. 700. Then in the early 1000s a revolution in architecture appeared so suddenly, and in a style so radical, that it is impossible to imagine it happening without outside inspiration. The city of Paquimé began to take shape, an immense adobe pueblo with vast plazas, ceremonial ball courts, reservoirs, and an engineered water system of aqueducts, storm drains, and even sewers. By the time Paquimé was complete, it had residential towers that may have risen as high as six or seven stories, and it sprawled over 88 acres.

The late archaeologist Charles DiPeso, who virtually adopted Paquimé as his life's work, placed its

The planting stick, or "dibble," is about three feet long and sharpened on one end. This simple tool was used universally by primitive farmers. JERRY JACKA

(PRECEDING PAGE 95) A Mogollon pottery fetish displays body paint commonly used as decoration by that culture. JERRY JACKA
(LEFT) Mimbres black-on-white bowl. This exceptional style of Mogollon pottery flourished between A.D. 1025 to 1150 in the Mimbres River valley of southwestern New Mexico. DAVID MUENCH

urban florescence at A.D. 1060. An Anasazi building boom at Chaco Canyon erupted at almost exactly the same time, which has more than just a whiff of coincidence about it. If this time sequence is right, it seems likely that some traders, priests, or visionaries from a more advanced Mesoamerican society had found their way into Mogollon and Anasazi territory, bringing revolutionary ideas about art, architecture, and perhaps the very composition of their culture.

Other archaeologists, however, recently have challenged DiPeso's chronology, moving up the rise of Paquimé almost 100 years to 1150. This would suggest that these two great trading centers of two diverse cultures arose from different inspirations.

The first Europeans to view the ruins of Paquimé flew into delirious romanticization, not archaeological pondering. Reported Baltasar de Obregón in 1584, "... this large city ... contains buildings that seemed to have been constructed by the ancient Romans. It is marvelous to look upon .... The houses contain large and magnificent patios paved with enormous and beautiful stones resembling jasper ...." Obregón's flight is understandable; Paquimé must have awed its contemporaries as well. In the Mogollon world, Paquimé was Manhattan, and everything else was, quite literally, the sticks — and the pits.

Archaeology can provide a vivid picture of life in Paquimé. It was the dominant trade center of the Southwest and one of the most urban pueblos anywhere, with a peak population of about 2,200. The Paquiméans produced copper bells, ceremonial ax heads, ornaments, and cloisonné. They imported and then raised brilliantly colored macaws, which they kept in rows of nesting pens still visible at the ruins today. Paquimé probably was the macaw capital of the Southwest, and the birds' plumage was traded for decorative or ceremonial use. The macaw merchants, wrote DiPeso, "would have attracted visitors not unlike a Venetian glass-blower's shop." They nearly invented the wheel, although they didn't realize it: the adobe macaw pens had round openings that were fitted with eggplant-shaped stones to plug the holes. It would have been a small step to the cartwheel and axle. But they had no domesticable animals to pull carts and, consequently, no real need for wheels.

Animal and human figures did serve in the Paquiméan imagination and religion. Effigy vessels were more prominent here than anywhere in the Southwest. Hand-molded bodies and faces of birds, snakes, lizards, felines, and people bulged from Paquimé pots. Some pot-people cradled babies, some smoked, and some fondled their genitals (Paquiméan potters were never prudish). Some pots exhibited two faces, recalling the Roman god Janus — and Obregón's observation that the city "seemed to have been constructed by the Romans."

Nothing about Paquimé was more amazing than its water system, a paragon of prehistoric

engineering. A canal brought fresh water from Vareleño spring in the volcanic foothills of the nearby Prieto Mountains. Stone-lined aqueducts roughly 10 inches wide and 10 inches deep cut across plazas and under walls to service the Paquimé condominiums. Some aqueducts terminated in plazas and ran downhill and out — baffling, until you realize they were storm drains. Rain pooling in the plazas, enclosed by buildings, would have melted the adobe foundations, inviting collapse.

Some of the channels were apparently used as sewers. DiPeso's monumental study in the 1960s and '70s found high levels of ammonium nitrogen, nitrates, and nitrites in the soil under them, telltale indicators of human or animal excrement. Lest anyone think too highly of the Paquiméans' civil engineering, DiPeso pointed out that the sewers

dumped their waste into a main aqueduct, rather seriously polluting the water supply for everyone downstream.

While the exact timelines of Paquimé and Chaco Canyon are currently in archaeological dispute, comparisons between the two are forever intriguing. They both had roads radiating from their respective pueblos, although those at Paquimé were not as grand as Chaco's. Both settlements required far more architectural planning and social control than any Southwestern pueblos before them. Both became centers for ceremony and trade. But distinct differences existed, too, in architecture, pottery, and ceremonial structures. And, of course, Chaco had no hydrological engineering inside the pueblos (nor, probably, enough water to make it possible).

About the same time that Paquimé's adobe foundations were being packed into place, another Mogollon nucleus in western New Mexico began producing a style of pottery that appears avant-garde even in the 20th century. Mimbres pottery had been evolving slowly for 800 years, from plain brownware through decorated redware. Then suddenly, shortly after A.D. 1000, the Mimbreño potters, possibly inspired by the artistic Hohokam on their western flank, began producing a spectacular black-on-white ware featuring a phantasmagoric menagerie of animal and humanesque images.

Pioneer archaeologist Jesse Fewkes believed the Mimbres pot-creatures represented mythological beings and narrative legends. In view of the complex mythology of modern Pueblo people, who include the Mimbres' descendants, Fewkes' theory seems highly plausible.

Most Mimbres pottery art was painted in black on the inner surfaces of wide bowls finished with a white slip. The images are organized masterfully in terms of their geometry; they express both grace and tension at the same time. Some are entirely geometric abstractions, dramatic compositions of scrolls, pinwheels, hatched triangles, zigzags checkerboards, and lampshades. Some are entirely pictorial or narrative, depicting, for example, hunting or fishing scenes. Many others

Text continued on page 104

(LEFT) The final incarnation of Paquimé did not evolve haphazardly, but was carefully planned, with its underground hydrological systems laid out before the adobe village was built.

(ABOVE) The T-shaped portal is a prominent feature at Paquimé, used for windows and large public doorways. Some suggest it indicates specific rooms that were used for religious ceremonies. BOTH BY DAVID BURCKHALTER

Mimbres artists painted startlingly beautiful stylized designs on nine- to ten-inch-diameter pottery bowls and jars. Their most interesting works interpreted nature with fluid lines and geometric shapes while their human subjects generally were rendered rather plainly.

(ABOVE, LEFT TO RIGHT)
Two clowns, part human and part turtle or insect, cavort across a bowl. A menacing man in a kilt carries a snare. Symmetrical feather design still used on Pueblo pottery today. Two imaginative creatures, part bird, part fish, display geometric decoration.

(BELOW, LEFT TO RIGHT)

Two dancers, one with an animal head, carry rattles and staffs with feathers attached. Alongside stand an animal and fish combination and a lizard. A man with three snares has tied three birds to a fence or cage while two birds walk toward a gourd. Polychrome geometric designs decorate this seed jar. Two geometrically patterned deer balance on a polychrome bowl.

PHOTOGRAPHS BY
JERRY JACKA

Text continued from page 101

are elaborate fusions of abstraction and representation. Many seem (to us) whimsical, some comical, and a few even frightening — one famous Mimbres bowl vividly depicts a human decapitation scene. Wherever animals appear, they are usually highly stylized and decorated, their very forms evoking a mood. A water bird may appear dark and sinister, a scorpion may be encrusted with gay tattoos and wearing a bemused "who, me?" expression. Sometimes they are transmogrified into mythological creatures, such as a giant catfish with human feet and hands. Human forms, oddly, are usually undecorated and inexpressive silhouettes.

What did it all mean? In some way, these images probably were icons of an ideology that was deeply engaged with Nature at the spiritual level. Perhaps the Mimbres had an understanding of their world that surpasses our own. That would explain why much of their art, captivating though it may be, utterly bewilders us.

Not many Mimbres bowls survive intact. They are typically found with a hole punched in the center. The usual explanation is that this hole was to release the "spirit" of the bowl, but this also is only conjecture. Mimbres black-on-white-style potmaking evaporated around A.D. 1150, so no tradition survives to help explain it.

Just as perplexing is another unique Mogollon undertaking that began around A.D. 1250 on a rim of volcanic rock overlooking the Round Valley of the Little Colorado River: Casa Malpais.

This "House of the Badlands," to translate its Spanish name, had been known and periodically explored (and pothunted) since 1883, but not until 1990 did archaeologists discover its most startling secrets. Casa Malpais was a special place and probably served as a central religious focus for the surrounding district. On the stepped talus of the basalt-covered mesa were rooms that contained ceramics that almost appeared to be new; rooms that suggested societies might have met there; and a large, square great kiva. Kivas of this size probably were gathering places for ceremonies on an intercommunity level. A

(ABOVE) A metate and mano for grinding corn and a corrugated pottery cooking bowl were common household items for the Mogollon who built Casa Malpais.

(RIGHT) A three-inch-long stone pipe and bone whistle from Casa Malpais. Native tobacco was a common prehistoric crop.

(FACING PAGE) The distinctive Mogollon square kiva at Casa Malpais, near Springerville, Arizona, has a built-in bench along the wall — a typical Anasazi feature. It may have been in this area that the kachina cult had its beginning.

(FOLLOWING PANEL) Escudilla Mountain in the White Mountains of eastern Arizona south of Casa Malpais. The Mogollon farmed, hunted, and gathered throughout the scenic forested mountain country along the Arizona-New Mexico border.

PHOTOGRAPHS BY JERRY JACKA

104

scarcity of true habitation rooms supports this theory. And finally, in a series of natural caverns in the basalt underneath the pueblo, the inhabitants of Casa Malpais had built underground stone walls and even roofs to form sealed burial crypts.

That discovery made the front page of *The New York Times* and rocked the archaeological establishment at least as dramatically as had Haury's Mogollon findings 54 years earlier. Many archaeologists felt that calling them burial "crypts" was sensationalist, implying (as had Obregón) that the people of Malpais were some sort of New World Romans. They weren't, but Casa Malpais was definitely a special place, its purpose as puzzling as Chaco Canyon.

And as if all this were not controversy enough, archaeologists disagree on whether the pueblo was Mogollon, Anasazi, or a composite. Two architectural cultures mingle in it: the pueblo walls look like Anasazi masonry, but the great kiva is square, which identifies it as Mogollon — and, maddeningly, it features an Anasazi-style bench along its inside perimeter.

This cultural mixture, however, is typical of the late Mogollon. Many sites, such as those at Gila Cliff Dwellings National Monument, look suspiciously like Anasazi, and ever since Haury's designation of the Mogollon culture, archaeologists have argued over Mogollon-Anasazi interaction. Who absorbed whom? For those who lived here, it apparently didn't matter. Hopi and Zuni today claim both cultures among their ancestors, and there is plenty of evidence to support each of these claims. The archaeologists working at Casa Malpais brought both Hopi and Zuni elders to look at the petroglyphs prolifically scattered around the pueblo. Both could "read" them. But as one might expect, they interpreted them differently.

VISITING THE MOGOLLON WORLD

PAQUIMÉ (CASAS GRANDES RUINS)

Despite the occasional vexations of a trip to Mexico, anyone intrigued by Southwestern prehistory needs to visit Paquimé. While it raises more questions about the Mogollon and their influential visitors than it answers, it also raises one's regard for this vanished culture. Whatever the inspiration for Paquimé, it was a uniquely ambitious city.

The ruins lie about four miles (six kilometers) southwest of the modern town of Nuevo Casas Grandes, Chihuahua, a prosperous agricultural center founded and still influenced by Mormons. The trip southeast from the border at Douglas, Arizona, is 135 miles, most of which is on Mexican Route 2, a lonely and badly maintained road that presents more potholes than pavement. Better routes cross the border at Columbus, New Mexico (112 miles), and El Paso, Texas (208 miles). Nuevo Casas Grandes has several good motels, most lining Avenida Benito Juarez, the main highway through town.

The ruin is open every day "except when extremely wet," according to the caretaker. Visitors are free to wander through all the excavated rooms and into the ball courts, reservoirs, and atop the mounds. Unfortunately, there are no guides, interpretive exhibits, or signs in either Spanish or English to help

Human effigy jar from Paquimé. Judging from illustrations and from the amount of pigment found at the ruins, facial painting was quite common among the Mogollon.
GILL C. KENNY

explain this vast ruin, so some preparation is essential to getting the most out of it. Charles DiPeso's exhaustive eight-volume *Casas Grandes* is in many Southwestern libraries, and the Amerind Foundation in Dragoon, Arizona, has a provocative display of Casas Grandes effigy vessels. The better motels in Nuevo Casas Grandes give out free brochures that provide some background and a site plan of the ruins.

Las Ruinas de Casas Grandes (Paquimé), Nuevo Casas Grandes, Chihuahua, Mexico.

GILA CLIFF DWELLINGS NATIONAL MONUMENT

Nowhere does Mogollon architecture look more like Anasazi than at Gila Cliff Dwellings. Six natural alcoves in the canyon wall 175 feet above the Gila River shelter about 40 rooms made of volcanic tuff blocks cemented with adobe mortar. The first dwelling encountered on the mile-long loop trail has a T-shaped door, the same prominent form seen at Paquimé 200 miles to the south, and at Pueblo Bonito 200 miles to the north. Like the cliff pueblos of the Kayenta and Mesa Verde Anasazi, the Gila Cliff Dwellings appear to have a defensive posture. One can intellectualize about the advantages the alcove provides – protection from wind, rain, and snow; cool shade in summer; warm southern exposure in winter — still, modern visitors find it hard to imagine why else the inhabitants endured the 175-foot climb up from their fields and the river's water supply.

Like spectacular pueblos of the Anasazi cultural sunset, the Gila Cliff Dwellings were occupied briefly. Construction began in A.D.1276, and they were abandoned 30 to 40 years later.

The pueblo was first surveyed by Adolph Bandelier in 1884, and became a national monument in 1907 — five years before New Mexico statehood. The monument is 44 miles north of Silver City, New Mexico, at the end of a corkscrewing (paved) mountain road. The drive is lovely, but will take at least 90 minutes. Check with the monument for closing times and winter road conditions before starting.

Gila Cliff Dwellings National Monument, Route 11, Box 100, Silver City, NM 88061.

CASA MALPAIS ARCHAEOLOGICAL PARK

This unique site is being developed by the small town of Springerville, Arizona, which views it not only as a cultural resource but also as a promising tourist attraction. The burial crypts are not open to visitors now and never will be.

Visitors nevertheless find other matters to wonder upon. Why was Casa Malpais, built over five terraces on the side of a basaltic hill, apparently not concerned about defense? It easily could have been assaulted from below or surprised from above — and it was occupied during a time of apparent tensions in the region, about A.D. 1250 to 1400. Archaeologists excavating and stabilizing the ruin have guessed the reason through their own experiences. In winter and spring, the top of the hill is indeed assaulted — by frigid 60-mph winds. In summer, the air in the Little Colorado floodplain below is clotted with biting insects. Casa Malpais, sited between the floodplain and hilltop, appears to occupy the most practical and livable site in the area, then or now.

There is no visitors center at the site yet, but people may take self-guided tours of the aboveground ruins. Check in first at park headquarters in the center of town, 318 Main Street.

Casa Malpais Archaeological Park, P.O. Box 390, Springerville, AZ 85398.

This corrugated Mogollon pot stands 6.5 inches high.
JERRY JACKA

HOHOKAM

. . . IRRIGATORS OF THE DESERT

Summer comes to the Sonoran Desert, broiling and parching the land and its inhabitants with a savagery that seems determined to drive out nearly every living thing. Turkey vultures aimlessly cruise the updrafts rising off the simmering sand, waiting for heat or thirst to kill their lunch for them. The sun's light and heat strike exposed skin with such ferocity that they seem to exert unbearable pressure; the only reasonable response is to find or invent shelter. Reptiles, rodents, and humans not suffering from dementia are inside, spending the long days under rocks or deep in burrows — or in refrigerated malls. Arroyos creasing the land have been desiccated for months; the Salt River Valley, where modern Phoenix resides, sees only half an inch of rain throughout an average April, May, and June. Saguaros undergo their seasonal starvation diet, slimming like anorexics as they use up internal stores of water during the first half of the summer.

It looks like an impossible environment for an ancient civilization without cold drinks, municipal water tanks, or trucks to ferry in food from more moderate climates. Exactly the opposite is true. The Sonoran Desert was the most favorable of all the environments in the prehistoric Southwest. It provided the longest growing season, the most reliable rivers, and the greatest variety of edible native plants. If summers

were long and torrid, well, they were no worse than winters for the upland Anasazi, Mogollon, and Sinagua — and the people of the desert ate much better.

These people, who we call the Hohokam, occupied the desert basins cradling present-day Phoenix, Tucson, and much of the land 50 to 100 miles out in each direction. Archaeologists estimate that at their population peak in the 1200s, these early people numbered 20,000 to 50,000 in the Hohokam heartland around Phoenix alone.

Although their architecture would not have impressed an Anasazi, their civil engineering astounds even modern Americans. They dug well over 500 miles of irrigation canals in the Salt River Valley, the remnants of which were still visible in 1867 when a prospector and speculator named Jack Swilling rode into the valley and realized that this desert had once been farmed and could be again. With that idea, Phoenix was born.

The Hohokam story begins at a vague date among people of disputed lineage. Their "origin" might have been as early as A.D. 1 or as late as A.D. 300. These industrious people may have been Mesoamerican migrants who brought the basic knowledge of irrigation with them when they arrived from the south. Or indigenous Archaic hunters and gatherers who learned irrigation and pottery by word that filtered up from the south along trade routes. Current thinking favors the latter.

One reason Hohokam archaeology is blurry is that dendrochronology does not work with the desert mesquite, ironwood, and paloverde that the Hohokam favored for their fires and buildings. Recently some fir and pine beams were discovered in Hohokam houses north of Tucson, and one sliver of Hohokam chronology fell into place. While our understanding of Hohokam comings and goings is not as accurate as that of the Anasazi, improvements in chronology are occurring through the use of high-tech tools, such as radiocarbon dating (measuring the amount of low-level radioactive carbon that remains in old organic material) and paleomagnetic dating (measuring the change in the angle of declination between magnetic and true north in rocks taken from Hohokam firepits).

This carved slate palette was once used to mix pigment for face painting.
JERRY JACKA

For the first several hundred years, the Hohokam clustered in small villages of pithouses, sometimes encircling a central plaza. Around A.D. 750 came ball courts, the first great communal innovation, something that has intrigued and frustrated investigators since the advent of Hohokam archaeology in the 1920s.

There are at least 200 ball courts in Arizona alone — if that is what they are. The evidence is compelling. Mesoamericans had been playing ball games perhaps as early as 1200 B.C. Invading Spaniards documented one game in the 1500s, a soccerlike sport the Aztecs called *ulamaliztli*. Players struck the ball with their shoulders, hips, or knees, trying to knock it through one or two stone rings. In the courts of northwest Mexico and Hohokam country, the rings were replaced with stone markers in the floor.

The Mesoamerican game was associated with their gods, who presumably played it in heavenly courts, and also with gambling — sometimes entire kingdoms may have been won or lost in the games. Archaeologists suspect the Mesoamerican version was sometimes a ceremonial substitute for warfare with the winners "banking" wealth or territory. Other games were symbolic representations of the movements of the sun and moon, which were related to agricultural fertility. In Mesoamerica these games were serious indeed, sometimes ending with the sacrificial killing of a team captain in order for the celestial cycles to continue.

The Arizona courts were usually oval pits lined by embankments, presumably for spectators, and had a plastered floor set with stone markers. They varied in size, but among the largest, at the village of Snaketown along the Gila River, was a court 200 feet long, 100 feet wide, and 19 feet deep. Investigations elsewhere have turned up three small balls made from the rubber of the guayule plant. Although not actually found in courts, they are generally taken as proof that the Hohokam did play some sort of ball game. A stone ball was found in the court at Pueblo Grande in Phoenix, and it is assumed similar balls were used at other sites as well. While the Hohokam games are believed to have been similar to those in Mexico, the comparison is by

Carved stone mortars and a pestle were used for grinding red hematite and green chrysacolla pigment.
JERRY JACKA

118

inference. Unlike the Mesoamerican game, there is no hard evidence that Hohokam contests ended with sacrificial killings.

Whatever games were played in these arenas, they had important ceremonial significance. They may also have had something to do with cooperation among neighboring villages or perhaps different cultures (a number of ball courts appeared in Sinagua territory just after the eruption of Sunset Crater). What intrigues archaeologists is the apparent demise of the courts and games between A.D. 1050 and 1200. As the courts were abandoned, more and more platform mounds appeared and became the most prominent feature of Hohokam civic architecture. The shift apparently reflected profound changes in the ceremonial life and even the very structure of Hohokam society. Possibly the mound-builders and ball players were two competitive cults, or perhaps the disappearing ball court network meant that cooperation was breaking down and more serious competition was developing.

The mounds themselves evolved over time. The earliest were small, low, slope-sided ovals built of trash and fill dirt; they may have functioned as dance platforms. Later they became larger and more imposing, none more so than the Pueblo Grande mound in southeast Phoenix. Twenty feet high, 300 feet long, and 150 feet across, this mammoth mound started as two smaller piles that expanded and became a single mound comprising nearly 900,000 cubic feet of fill. At one time it had more than two dozen rooms on top of it. Later mounds also featured high adobe walls, which might have kept unauthorized eyes from watching mound-top activities. All this suggests privileged use in contrast to the populist ritual of ball games in a sunken arena. If the mounds were centers for village leaders or religious societies, ordinary people would not have shared in the arcane knowledge, and perhaps the wealth, except during ceremonial occasions.

The mounds were being rebuilt and expanded continuously over the centuries. The size of the task was put into perspective when archaeologists calculated that if 100 people had worked on the Pueblo Grande mound for one month a year, it would have taken them 24 years to build. What would convince or compel a work force to take on this job and compromise their more practical daily survival tasks, such as farming, hunting, wood gathering, and maintaining their own homes? We can only speculate. What seems obvious is that by the 1200s Hohokam society had organized itself into a management and labor arrangement, and the main purpose was to operate one of the most ambitious irrigation systems in the ancient North American world.

The well-dressed Hohokam probably wore a kilt, face paint, a bone hairpin, and shell jewelry. When traveling long distances, he carried a gourd canteen with a corncob plug and wore yucca-fiber sandals when on rough ground. On smooth trails he went barefoot.
ILLUSTRATION BY
GARY BENNETT

The agricultural success of the Hohokam culture allowed enough leisure time for the manufacture of an impressive variety of jewelry. **(TOP, LEFT)** This turquoise necklace is made up of 1,212 beads and 240 pendants. **(ABOVE)** A shell artistically etched with fermented saguaro juice. **(LEFT AND RIGHT)** Earrings were made from turquoise and hematite. **(BELOW)** Pitch from desert plants bonded a mosaic of turquoise and hematite stones to a shell pendant.

A wide variety of shells for jewelry was acquired during treks to the Sea of Cortes and from trade with coastal tribes.

(ABOVE AND RIGHT) Glycymeris shells were the dominant type of shell crafted into bracelets, and a host of other shell species were made into necklaces, pendants, rings, earrings, bandoliers of tinklers, and fetishes.

(BELOW, RIGHT) Holes in beads, pendants, and other jewelry items were made with a pump drill which used stone tips, similar in shape to small arrowheads, as drill bits.

PHOTOGRAPHS BY
JERRY JACKA

Although a small canal in Tempe has been dated to about A.D. 50, the Hohokam began to dredge large canals around A.D. 600, extending tendrils of their culture into the desert basin on either side of the Salt River. Main canals ran from four to 15 miles; each complete canal system, including the large "mains," medium "distributors," and smaller "laterals" averaged 34 miles. Some of the main canals were 40 feet wide and 10 feet deep. The Hohokam scale corresponds with the modern Salt River Project canals, which supply irrigation water to 180,000 homes and farms in metropolitan Phoenix today.

Why were the main canals so big? Some archaeologists wonder if they might have been used for transportation, although only one remnant of what may have been a raft has ever been found. It is possible that Hohokam agronomists found their croplands becoming increasingly saline after hundreds of years of irrigation, eventually turning sterile. That would have made it necessary to cultivate fresh land regularly. But after A.D. 1100, the primary driving force for the canal system was the population boom. The Hohokam were planning for an increasingly urbanized future. By continually adding new canal systems, they could cultivate more land for more people.

In some way, platform mounds and the canal systems were linked. Village clusters were spaced about three miles apart along the canals, and those with the largest mounds rose near the headgates of the main canals. This settlement pattern appears to have been the architecture of an administrative hierarchy to control water distribution and manage maintenance, repairs, and new construction.

Among all the prehistoric cultures of the Southwest, the Phoenix Hohokam may have achieved the highest level of material organization. In *Cadillac Desert*, a monumental book about water use and abuse in the American West, author Marc Reisner observed that most of the world's early great civilizations arose on the prosperity

Artist's rendering of Pueblo Grande, in Phoenix, circa A.D. 1350. Located at the head of the Salt River canal system, it was among the Hohokam culture's most important and influential communities.
ILLUSTRATION BY JON JOHA

disputes over water rights among upstream and downstream irrigators could not have been much different from today's.

While the farmers and lawyers fussed along the Salt and Gila rivers in central Arizona, a less complex Hohokam life style evolved to the south around Tucson and the San Pedro River Valley to its east. Southern Arizona had more rainfall (in modern times, 12 inches annually in Tucson as compared to 7.5 in Phoenix). These Hohokam practiced nonirrigation farming. They constructed check dams across arroyos, created small terraces, and through numerous other techniques managed to coax enough water onto their fields to grow most of the same crops as along the Salt and Gila: corn, several varieties of beans, squash, and cotton. They also cultivated native plants that required almost no attention. Agave, for example, was important for its leaves (cordage material) and "hearts" (baked for food). Irrigation canals tapped some of their rivers, but not anywhere near the scale

irrigation provided, and then grew into Byzantine complexity because of it.

To bring off the feat [irrigation] demanded tremendous collective will: discipline, planning, a sense of shared goals. To sustain it required order, which led to the creation of powerful priesthoods, of bureaucracies. Irrigation invited large concentrations of people because of all the food; it probably demanded such concentrations because of all the work. Out of this, cities grew. Work became specialized. There had to be engineers, builders, architects, farmers — probably even lawyers, for the

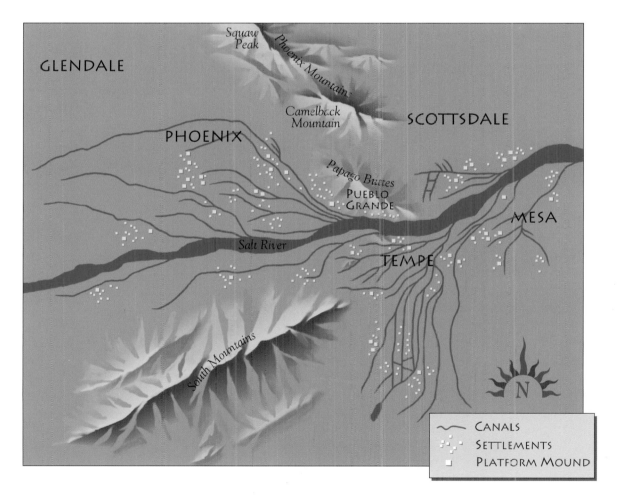

(TOP) Pueblo Grande Ruin today. Note modern canal in the background. DAVID BURCKHALTER
(ABOVE) Based on a 1929 map by Omar A. Turney and updated to include current information, the above illustration shows the finely engineered Hohokam canal system in the Salt River valley included well over 500 miles of canals. ILLUSTRATION BY KEVIN KIBSEY

that developed in Phoenix. The Southern Hohokam built smaller-scaled mounds than Pueblo Grande and, because of their simpler life-style, might have maintained a less complex society. They built no more ball courts after A.D. 1100.

About this same time, piled rock walls called *trincheras* ("trenches" in Spanish) began to snake across Hohokam hillsides in southern Arizona and northern Mexico. Traditionally, archaeologists assumed they were fortifications, but that theory is shaky: at many trinchera sites the people lived at the foot of the hill, below the "protection" of the multiple rock walls.

Recent research has found that the hillsides tend to have more frost-free days, which builds a case for the walls as dams to trap runoff on terraced fields. But why were they three to five feet high? Did they have ceremonial functions? Speculation on the trincheras continues.

To modern eyes, agriculture without irrigation in the Sonoran Desert looks like a reckless adventure. Certainly there were years when crops failed. Ten inches of rain a year is a bare minimum for dry-land cultivation. (In the 50 years between 1940 and 1990, Tucson's precipitation fell below that minimum 19 times.) But this is deceptive. The desert is rich in native foods. About 425 edible species grow wild, and the Hohokam made excellent use of them. Mesquite trees grow bean pods every summer, even in an abnormally dry year, and they can be ground into a sweet flour for bread. The fruit of the saguaro cactus provides more calories per unit of dry weight than cultivated maize. Roasted cholla buds are more nutritious than cow's milk.

And when the rains did bless the fields, the warm land responded with not just one but two growing seasons in a year. This was, of course, especially true in irrigated areas. As much as common sense would like to argue otherwise, the Sonoran Desert — so parched and seemingly inhospitable on a 110-degree summer day — was the best place in the prehistoric Southwest to be a farmer.

Prehistoric hillside *trincheras*, piled rock walls, held soil and scarce rainwater. This type of Hohokam farming was common to the southern Arizona around modern-day Tucson.
P.K. WEIS

124

When Nature smiles and grants a people the luxury of dedicating less of their time to farming and food gathering, their arts and crafts blossom. This was another gift the generous desert gave the Hohokam, who were perhaps the most artistically expressive of all the Southwest's prehistoric people.

Only about seven to 10 percent of Hohokam pottery was decorated, but it was a very sophisticated form of art. From A.D. 700-900, red-on-buff Hohokam pottery sizzled with life as well as geometric designs. Painted lizards, turtles, snakes, birds, rabbits, deer, fish, and bugs paraded around pots and jugs and bowls either in whimsy or with incredible energy — depending, apparently, on the potter's mood.

A roadrunner would have its leg cocked in midstep; a snake might be painted in an errant slither that looks more mischievous than menacing. Some potters even indulged in Hohokam humor: a shard found at the Snaketown excavation depicts flute-playing cockroaches. Always the figures are simple and cartoonlike, but their freshness and spontaneity are endearing.

Human figures also dance across Hohokam pottery. Some archaeologists find it significant that they often appear in an unbroken line or circle, linked by their hands. Hohokam-style irrigation demanded cooperation among all the families and villages served by a canal, and hand-holding could well be a symbolic representation.

After A.D. 900 there was a smaller variety of life-forms that tended to be more stylized, and a greater percentage of the vessels had geometric designs. Interestingly, some of the dance figures appear with alternate images, perhaps male and female, during this time. By 1200, most pottery was an unpainted but lovely redware, intentionally smudged to black on the inside accompanied by accidental gray "fire cloud" spots on the outside.

Hohokam clays were inferior to those of the Anasazi, so the vessels broke easily. But nevertheless, their whimsical art

One of many designs perhaps symbolizing cooperation, people holding hands circle this Hohokam red-on-buff jar.
JERRY JACKA

The Hohokam painted loose designs on these effigy vessels and red-on-buff bowl.
JERRY JACKA

Functional plainware was the everyday pottery used by the Hohokam and accounted for nearly 90 percent of the vessels they made.
PHOTOGRAPHS BY
JERRY JACKA

was unique. Archaeologist Charles Avery Amsden once compared Hohokam and Anasazi potters, declaring that "the latter is a well-schooled draughtsman, the former an unschooled artist." The Anasazi would carefully paint the outline of a figure and fill it in; the Hohokam would loose a blob of pigment onto the surface and then tease it into its proper form.

Hohokam artists also became adept at working seashells acquired by trade from Pacific Coast or Sea of Cortes people. Several centuries before Europeans thought they invented acid etching, the Hohokam were applying designs to shells with an organic resist, then marinating the shells in a mild acid, perhaps fermented saguaro fruit juice. Thus etched with horned toads or exotic geometric designs, the shells were made into pendants, bracelets, rings, and even trumpets. The Hohokam did more engraving with stone tools than they did etching, but in both cases their jewelry, though very rare, became prized throughout the Southwest; a millennium later, excavators would find it in the remains of Mogollon and Anasazi villages.

Human effigies were formed in clay by Hohokam artists as fertility symbols, good luck charms, and toys.
JERRY JACKA

Hohokam architecture, with one surviving exception, was never as impressive as that of the Anasazi. Even after the pithouse era, the Hohokam did not attempt masonry (some stone was used at Pueblo Grande) but built their houses of adobe formed and packed by hand into monolithic walls. Without exterior plaster or eaves to divert rainwater, Hohokam home ownership was an exercise in relentless maintenance. People surely welcomed the rain on their crops, but they must have had mixed feelings as the same storms melted their houses.

The great anomaly in their architecture is Casa Grande (Spanish for "Big House"), a Hohokam high rise thrusting into the desert sky 40 miles southeast of Phoenix. Jesuit missionary Eusebio Kino, who was the first white man to stumble across the ruin, wrote in 1694 that it must have been built by the ancestors of Montezuma, who later were driven out by the Apaches and went on to found Teotihuacán, north of Mexico City. Kino was wrong on every point, but it is understandable that the sight of a prehistoric adobe tower four stories high inspired his imagination.

Built around A.D. 1350, Casa Grande was the highest expression — both literally and symbolically — of the Hohokam. Its first story is actually a platform mound five feet high. The three floors over it were divided into 11 rooms. A circular window high in the west wall aligns precisely with sunset at summer solstice, and an alignment on the east wall is a dawn marker for spring and fall equinox, confirming the building was used as an observatory. That Casa Grande had ceremonial significance there is no doubt. But what those ceremonies were no one may ever know, for like the Chaco Canyon great houses, Casa Grande is very good at expressing power and preserving secrets.

Hohokam culture began edging toward oblivion well before Casa Grande was built; by 1450 it barely existed. The large villages and great canal systems were history. The population shriveled to maybe a tenth of what it had been. The Hohokam cultural pulse went flat. But where did these people go?

Emil Haury, the dean of Hohokam archaeology, maintained throughout his long and distinguished career that the modern Akimel O'odham (Pima) and Tohono O'odham (Papago) tribes of Arizona are in fact the living Hohokam. In 1976 Haury summed up his convictions:

To assert that there was no connection between the Piman people and Hohokam requires the removal of the latter from the area by about A.D. 1450 and the introduction of the Pimans with an impressively similar lifeway almost immediately. Contacts in the 16th and 17th centuries by Europeans indicate that the Pimas were comfortably adjusted to their desert habitat, a "fit" that bespeaks a long residence rather than exceptional cultural adaptability.

(**ABOVE**) In addition to working with a variety of shells, Hohokam artists also carved pendants and figurines from stone. (**LEFT AND RIGHT**) Small horned toad and mountain sheep stone bowls were probably used as incense burners.

PHOTOGRAPHS BY JERRY JACKA

Casa Grande National Monument rises to four stories amid the cactus and creosote of the
Sonoran Desert along the Gila River. The roof is the second constructed over the adobe
structure to prevent it from melting back into the earth from which it was made.
Tom Danielsen

Haury and his disciples believed that the sophisticated engineering and civic systems of the Hohokam collapsed because they had grown too unwieldy to respond to problems, such as drought or flood. The survivors reverted to a simpler, less urban, less interdependent lifeway, which is what Father Kino encountered in 1694. The very name

"Hohokam," a Piman word, seems to confirm it. Hohokam was translated as "that which has perished" by ethnographer Frank Russell in 1905. Haury later provided a better translation: "all used up." A blown-out tire is "hokam;" a pile of discarded tires is "hohokam." In Piman thinking, the Hohokam culture hadn't worked and was all used up.

Some younger generation archaeologists are suspicious of Hohokam-Pima continuity. The most serious problem is context of language. Modern Akimel O'odham (Pima) and Tohono O'odham (Papago) speak a Uto-Aztecan tongue that stretches from Utah, Nevada, and Southern California through Arizona and some 600 miles south into Mexico. Since the Hohokam culture penetrated Mexico only slightly, they feel the Akimel O'odham and Tohono O'odham sound like Mexican newcomers who filled a void left by the departed Hohokam. Not so, say others, and they proceed to demonstrate a language corridor to prove their point.

The architectural record lobs another dart at Haury's connective theory. The late Hohokam were skilled at adobe construction; the early Pima threw dirt on their stick-and-straw roofs and waited for the rain. Surely the Hohokam, retreating from a complex civic structure

that no longer worked, would not have abandoned all the technology that made them comfortable.

When the Spaniards came to Arizona in the mid-1500s, they found some Pima using small-scale irrigation and others not. Along the Gila River, most Pima simply were allowing periodic high water levels from upstream rains to lap over the riverbanks and water their fields. The Spaniards were surprised at this capricious method of agriculture. Nevertheless, it worked.

If the Hohokam in fact departed, it probably was not a very dramatic diaspora. Some may have joined the Hopi melting pot on the Colorado Plateau; indeed the Hopi claim an affiliation based on oral legends. However it was that the Hohokam culture dribbled out of existence, it must have been an impoverished finale for a people of such striking accomplishments.

(**ABOVE**) Art imitates Hohokam life in this red-on-buff effigy of a potter.
(**RIGHT**) Hohokam "cigarettes" were reeds stuffed with tobacco and wrapped with cotton thread to insulate the fingers from the heat.
BOTH BY JERRY JACKA

VISITING THE HOHOKAM WORLD

CASA GRANDE RUINS NATIONAL MONUMENT

Situated on the flat creosote desert north of Coolidge, Arizona, this is the only Hohokam building of its kind left in existence, and it is tantalizing for the mysteries it harbors. Was it an observatory, an administrative hub, the center of an elite priesthood — or all of the above? Between A.D. 1300 and 1350, what compelled its builders to lug nearly 600 juniper, fir, and ponderosa pine logs about 30 miles from the Superstition Mountains to use as ceiling beams? And after all that work, why was it abandoned fewer than 100 years later?

At one time it apparently was part of a network of Casas Grandes. The Jesuit missionary Eusebio Kino reported in 1694 that to the east, north, and west there were "seven or eight more of these large old houses," some of which he claimed to have seen. Archaeologists have learned from excavations that there were apparently two big houses near the Salt River in what is now Phoenix, one of which was at Pueblo Grande. None of the remains, however, reveals what went on inside them.

The big house of Casa Grande is surrounded by the remnants of a scattering of ordinary small houses and a compound wall enclosing them. These adobe walls are now eroded into softly rounded, knee-high forms, strangely poignant symbols of the earth slowly reclaiming the efforts of mankind to reshape it. Other monument features include a ball court, platform mound (the latter is not accessible to the public), and museum.

The ruin was first stabilized in 1891 by Cosmos Mindeleff, working for the Smithsonian Institution. It was designated a National Monument in 1918.

Casa Grande Ruins National Monument, P.O. Box 518, Coolidge, AZ 85228.

(RIGHT)
A Hohokam red-on-buff human effigy face, broken from a larger figure, seems to peer from the past.
JERRY JACKA

PUEBLO GRANDE MUSEUM AND CULTURAL PARK

The city of Phoenix has owned Pueblo Grande, the preeminent Hohokam platform mound, since 1924. In 1964 the mound became a National Historic Landmark. A visit is helpful in understanding the character and ambitions of Hohokam culture. Several of the rooms atop the mound are visible, and numerous buildings that once surrounded it remain safely buried for future generations to study.

The Hohokam began occupation of the site before A.D. 500. Construction on the platform mound began about 1150 and expanded slowly over the course of 200 years. Its full scale — almost exactly the size of a modern football field — apparently was not part of the original plan; two smaller mounds eventually became one as "cells" were continually built and filled. Mound-top rooms were destroyed and new ones built in their places many times.

At its peak, the widely scattered village around Pueblo Grande occupied more than a square mile and included at least 1,000 people. Given the dramatic size of the mound and its location at the head of a great canal system in the Salt River Valley, it was surely among the most important communities of the Hohokam world.

The park has a museum with Hohokam artifacts, interpretive exhibits, a children's interactive exhibit, and ball court. It also offers periodic workshops and a summer children's program. The platform mound trail is wheelchair-accessible.

Pueblo Grande Museum, 4619 East Washington Street, Phoenix, AZ 85034.

CHAPTER FIVE

SALADO

... MYSTERY CULTURE OF THE TONTO BASIN

If the Sinagua are a mystery, the Salado are a mess. Colorado archaeologist Stephen H. Lekson used exactly that word, comparing the Salado to a pointillist painting. From a distance the images appear solid; at magnifying-glass range they're a mess.

Like the Mogollon, the Salado culture was first identified in the 1930s. The Salado buried rather than cremated their dead, built multistoried stone and adobe pueblos, and produced a dramatic and distinctive red, white, and black pottery later classified under the rubric of Salado polychrome. The exotic beauty of their ceramics, ironically, is partly to blame for the "mess" in the archaeological record: many of their villages were stripped by pothunters before archaeologists could begin serious study.

The Salado heartland was the Tonto Basin, 50 miles east of present-day Phoenix, an upper Sonoran Desert valley framed by the Sierra Anchas and Mazatzal Mountains and drained by Tonto Creek and the Salt River. It is a picturesque landscape, and it provided fertile farmland.

Harold S. Gladwin, who first identified the Salado culture, believed they were Mogollon and Anasazi who displaced an earlier Hohokam population. Outlining all the alternative theories since Gladwin's would create a colossal tangle, but, very briefly, the Salado have been accused of being Hohokam, a blend of Hohokam and Sinagua (whoever *they* were), and a stew of Hohokam, Mogollon, and Anasazi. As if this were not confusion enough, their polychrome pottery (so named because of the multicolored designs), or something strongly influenced by the Salado style, was traded as much as 350 miles to the east around present-day Roswell, New Mexico, and a similar style was crafted 300 miles south at Casas Grandes, Chihuahua, Mexico.

Is there any way to mop up the Salado mess? Perhaps yes. Some archaeologists propose that we view the Salado as a phenomenon rather than as an ethnic group. It might have been religious or political or both, and it spread across cultural lines much as the Reformation in Europe would do centuries later. The pottery formed its "signature." Salado polychromes were among the most widely traded, and cherished, of all the ceramics of the ancient Southwest.

Archaeologists dispute the Salado chronology, but some workable dates are A.D. 1150 to 1450. This would be a short life span for a culture, but a long one for a movement. Within this time frame we can see three polychrome styles develop, observe a frenzy of

(PRECEDING PAGE 131) A Salado polychrome effigy vessel found in the Tonto Basin east of Phoenix.

(LEFT) Like the sand sweeping over this shard of a broken Tonto polychrome human effigy vessel, time and pothunters have obscured the story of the Salado culture of central Arizona.
BOTH BY JERRY JACKA

(RIGHT) Because of its beauty, Salado pottery is in high demand and much of it has been excavated and sold to collectors, destroying or obscuring archaeological evidence that may have helped to unlock the secrets of their past. GEORGE H.H. HUEY

(FOLLOWING PANEL)
The incomparable view of the Tonto Basin, Roosevelt Lake, and the Sierra Ancha Mountains from Lower Ruin, Tonto National Monument.
JERRY SIEVE

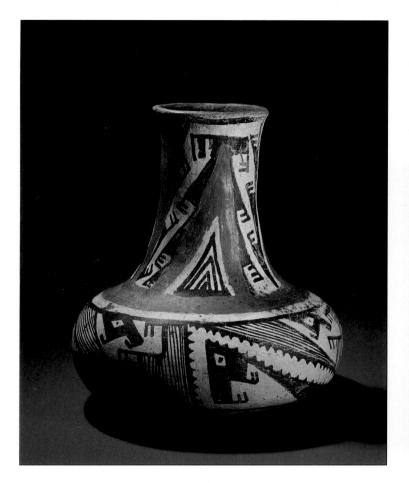

The Salado trademark was their exceptionally crafted and boldly painted polychrome and black-on-white pottery.
(LEFT) An 8 3/4-inch-tall long-neck Tonto polychrome vase. JERRY JACKA

(ABOVE) The Salado also traded widely. This Anasazi Snowflake black-on-white bowl which originated in the White Mountains, several hundred miles to the northeast, was found at a Salado site. JERRY JACKA
(BELOW) A Salado black-on-white jar from near Tonto National Monument resembles Anasazi black-on-white pottery. GEORGE H.H. HUEY

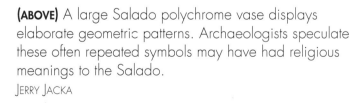

(ABOVE) A large Salado polychrome vase displays elaborate geometric patterns. Archaeologists speculate these often repeated symbols may have had religious meanings to the Salado.
JERRY JACKA

mound building in open country, and see the construction of cliff dwellings beginning around 1280.

Salado potters employed such an organized repertoire of geometric images that it is hard to imagine they didn't have specific, tangible meanings to people of the time. Certain motifs reappear time after time, on bowl after bowl, across centuries and tens of thousands of square miles. There are interlocking scrolls, both square and curled; stepped triangles; serrated rails; squares with a tiny "eye" in the middle; and a three-feather abstraction that still appears on Hopi pottery today. The patterns are bold and complicated, often symmetrical but with their balance broken by an inexplicable (to us) alteration of one figure. The color scheme varies according to the three styles — Pinto, Gila, and Tonto polychrome — but always incorporates red, black, and white. Gila polychrome is distinctive in that it has a band of paint called a "lifeline" around the rim, but a narrow gap or break is almost always left in it.

It is likely that Salado people understood the meaning of these images. Further it may be that the decorations were religious symbols or icons related to rain and crop fertility or society or ethnic affiliations expressed in design form. These were the most crucial concerns of all Southwestern people of A.D.

(RIGHT) Squatting comfortably, a stoic Salado effigy vessel with face and body paint endures the centuries.
JERRY JACKA

1250. Nothing else explains the consistency of the Salado artists' "vocabulary" quite as well.

As striking and intriguing as the ceramics are, the Salado platform mounds are yielding a more definitive story about the complexity of Salado village life. About 20 have been found in the Tonto Basin, the earliest constructed about A.D. 1280. These were enormous structures of earth and stone, 10 to 12 feet high, almost as large as half a modern football field. Building these mounds would have required a lot of human sweat, often more than was available in the little villages surrounding them. That implies that the mounds were built with coerced labor, or, more likely, they were ceremonial centers and work on them was obligatory as membership in certain societies or kin groups. Doubtlessly the mounds attracted a regional community.

At this writing, archaeologists from Arizona State University are conducting an eight-year, $10 million dig in the Tonto Basin, hoping to expose more mysteries of the Salado phenomenon to the desert sunlight and modern understanding. Glen Rice, archaeologist and senior principal investigator, has observed that numerous interpretations about the mounds are developing as work on these unique features of the past continues. In the

(RIGHT, CLOCKWISE FROM TOP) An argillite mountain lion, unidentified steatite animal, a steatite bird, and an argillite duck are examples of the Salado carved stone fetishes found in the Tonto Basin.
JERRY JACKA

March 1992 issue of *Arizona Highways* magazine, Peter Aleshire wrote that the key to the Salado riddle may lie in understanding two sites: the 700-year-old Pillar Mound, which was abandoned after a flood destroyed nearby irrigation works; and Schoolhouse Mound, which reached its peak of activity nearly 100 years later.

Pillar is the oldest of five mound sites ASU crews have studied to date; its construction marks the dawn of the distinct Salado culture. A lack of routine household debris suggests no one actually lived there, so the site could have been an ancient temple to the sun.

The vital clue is a series of tall stone pillars that did more than support the roof. One chilly December morning a few days after winter solstice, field director David Jacobs observed that light and shadows from the pillars and doorways lined up in a curious pattern. Subsequent measurements confirmed they formed a winter solstice marker. Six months later, the summer solstice worked its magic in the ruins as well. Centuries ago priests must have watched as the morning sun crested distant ridges. Then, as now, a dagger of light crept through the doorway onto the back wall and slowly lengthened downward until it rested briefly on the floor, perhaps illuminating a tableau of sacred objects. The harbinger of the seasons once again had come to its proper place.

A small clay bear fetish excavated at the Tonto Basin digs.

A very different series of events seems to have taken place at Schoolhouse Mound. Schoolhouse was an incredible 300-yard-long L-shaped mound, and its 115 rooms may have housed 200 people. One after another of these rooms had large vessels, giant baskets, and special "granaries" made of woven branches plastered with mud. To archaeologists this shows more than a clever system of food storage; it provides insight into the economy of the time.

One cannot visit the Tonto Basin and not be impressed by Salado ingenuity. Every three to five miles along the river they built a platform mound to anchor a canal system. In all they irrigated some 2,000 acres of corn and beans. Other "rural" settlements on the flanks of the valley harvested agave, prickly pear, and saguaro fruit. Altogether the basin may have supported 10,000 people. An "elite" administrative group that could control surpluses and direct the mass

(ABOVE) Salado red plainware pottery fills a sunlit doorway at Pillar Mound. The pillars and doorways were arranged to function as a calendar. At winter and summer solstices the rising sun's rays threw a thin dagger of light across the floor and up the back wall. The solar alignment and the lack of hearths and household artifacts lead archaeologists to speculate that Pillar Mound was a religious center.

(RIGHT) Bass Point on the banks of manmade Roosevelt Lake is one of several Salado culture platform mounds excavated by Arizona State University.

PHOTOGRAPHS BY JERRY JACKA

At several platform mounds in the Tonto Basin,
archaeologists painstakingly unearth the secrets of the past.
(ABOVE, LEFT) Dale Gerken excavates a group of large storage ollas at the Schoolhouse Point
site. The Salado of the Tonto Basin had incredible food storage capabilities, warehousing
enough reserves for their villages to survive several years of drought.
(ABOVE, RIGHT) Alongside cobbled foundations for granaries, Wallace Pottle takes samples
of a hearth for archaeomagnetic-dating purposes.
(BELOW) Artist's rendition of what life was like at a Salado platform mound.
ILLUSTRATION BY BILL AHRENDT

(**ABOVE**) An aerial view of excavations in progress at Schoolhouse Point Mound.
(**BELOW**) Trowel in hand, Patrice Bamat excavates a room at Cline Terrace Mound. The work has
exposed a rock wall that shows an Anasazi-influenced style of masonry.

PHOTOGRAPHS BY
JERRY JACKA

labor required by this increasingly complex society could have lived at Schoolhouse.

The first appearance of the mounds corresponds suspiciously to the arrival of the great drought of A.D. 1276 to 1299. Coincidence? Not too likely. Assume that the beginning of an administrative hierarchy already existed among the Salado because someone in authority had to organize the mound building. When hard times arrived, a way was needed to preserve prosperity. So the idea of the mounds as ceremonial temples to make rain was promoted, thereby enlisting the labor to build them. Phoenix City Archaeologist Todd Bostwick theorized that Southwestern cultures have long associated clouds and rain with mountains; therefore the mounds could have been symbolic "mountains."

It is also possible that the elite then moved onto the mounds — as the priestly aristocracy, only they had access to the knowledge of how to encourage rain — and that there they enjoyed a privileged life. ASU archaeologists have found five times the grain storage capacity per house on the mounds than in the flatlands. Discarded animal bones show that the mound people dined on deer while the common folk gnawed rabbit. The Salado may have been unique in the Southwest in having an upper class. "Archaeologists generally struggle to demonstrate the existence of a privileged elite," Rice explained. "Here, we just had it handed to us."

Was it also coincidence that cliff dwellings appeared in Salado territory at about the same time? Not if the sites were defensive. The more stratified a society becomes, the more potential it has for organized violence. On the other hand, sheltered alcove architecture could simply have been introduced by Anasazi immigrants. Indeed, mounds, pithouses, and structures associated with outlying fields, all in open indefensible areas, housed thousands while a relatively few families lived in the cliff dwellings. Perhaps they were all just part of a large subsistence system. As one would expect of a great cultural gathering — if that is what the Salado phenomenon truly was — architecture logically assumed several different forms.

The Salado walked away — or perhaps "ran" is a better word — from their homeland and scattered in the mid-to-late 1400s. ASU investigators found that they left behind not only large possessions, such as storage pots, but also small, easily portable valuables, such as axes, knives, and religious paraphernalia. "People clearly migrated out suddenly and didn't take much with them," Rice said. "Many rooms were burned. It could have been ceremonial burning; we can't necessarily say it was warfare."

Only two Salado ruins are accessible to the public, but both are spectacular — as is the pottery in the museum displays beside them.

A Salado builder left the impressions of his fingers in a mud wall of a Tonto Basin platform mound nearly 700 years ago. JERRY JACKA

The real intrigue lies in the Salado themselves, a people whose culture is only gradually coming into focus through the archaeologists' work in the Tonto Basin. Rice recalled the "quasi-mystical" moment when he found a perfect palm print on one of those Salado pillars.

"We aren't just studying pots and mud," he said.

(LEFT) Sunrise streams into a hallway at Lower Ruin, Tonto National Monument. The Salado culture thrived in the Tonto Basin while other cultures around them were declining. Speculations on what finally caused the demise of the Salado and the rapid abandonment of the region range from disease to overpopulation to hostilities.
JERRY SIEVE

PREHISTORIC CALENDARS

In prehistoric times, just as now, it was essential to determine the seasons — the people needed to know when to plant their crops. But the calendars of A.D. 1250 included much more information than that. Typically they noted such events as winter solstice, spring and fall equinox, and summer solstice. From those events they could count off the days, or perhaps the moon's phases, to establish exact ceremonial times.

Dr. Robert A. Preston, an astronomer at the Jet Propulsion Laboratory and his wife, Ann, a sculptor at Art Center, both in Pasadena, California, have discovered more than 75 examples of solstice events at numerous petroglypyh sites around Arizona. The Prestons determined that certain rock art images, predominantly spirals and circles, serve to mark solar sites. Typically, a sunlit image or shadow interacts with the center or edge of a spiral or circle. One of the more impressive calendric petroglyph sites the Prestons have identified is a cavelike rock shelter in the Petrified Forest which contains three spiral and two circular petroglyphs. All five symbols display the described sunlight interactions on the solstices. These and other findings are convincing proof that certain rock art was employed by prehistoric people as calendric markers.

A variety of measuring techniques was used. Noting the exact location of the sun on the horizon during dawn prayers might have been one of them. The Hohokam at Casa Grande used an alignment of small holes through the thick adobe walls of the Big House which, at equinox, allowed a spot of light to appear on an interior surface. The Salado people at Pillar Mound constructed a doorway that functioned in a similar manner with a sliver of light during winter and summer solstice. Countless other solar alignment sites still function perfectly as sunlit images and shadows meaningfully touch petroglyphs scratched onto rocky surfaces more than 600 years ago.

Equinoxes
It is believed that Casa Grande was, among other things, an astronomical observatory. An alignment of holes through four-foot-thick walls supports this theory. Shortly after dawn on spring and fall equinoxes, the rising sun shines through an outer portal. Shown here entering the second opening, a spot of light will momentarily appear on a wall of the innermost room. JERRY JACKA

Winter Solstice
At Wupatki National Monument, a pointed shadow forms when the midday sun of winter solstice first comes around the edge of a rock surface. Over a period of about 15 minutes the shadow shortens and the tip, moving left to right, brushes the top edge of the 20-inch spiral without entering it.
ROBERT PRESTON

Equinoxes
At spring and fall equinoxes, sunlight passes through the entrance of a cave at Petrified Forest National Park and falls on a petroglyph-covered rock. At the moment of sunset, the shadow from the entrance roof is perfectly tangent to a circle and adjacent spiral.
ROBERT AND ANN PRESTON

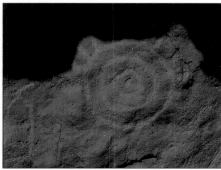

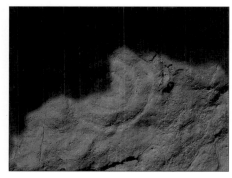

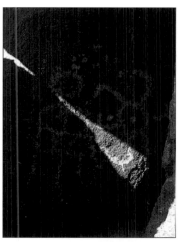

Winter Solstice
In northern Arizona a shadow descends and touches the top of a petroglyphic set of concentric circles with radiating sunlike rays. The shadow slowly moves from left to right and continues to touch the top of the circle without entering it while the point of the shadow pierces the left side of the glyph and strikes the center dot. The sequence takes about two hours.
ROBERT PRESTON

Summer and Winter Solstices
(ABOVE, LEFT) Along the Gila River southwest of Phoenix, an alignment performs multiple tasks. During summer solstice, a pointed sunlit image works from the top down: as the sun passes overhead, the sunlit point brushes the right side of a petroglyph circle without entering it. The tip then separates, passes through the small cross, and disappears. The remainder of the sunlit point, meanwhile, sweeps across the sunlike glyph, and the trailing edge traces down the right side of the sun symbol and disappears.
(ABOVE, RIGHT) During winter solstice, the same alignment works with pointed sunlit images that move from left to right: the trailing point of a sunlit image brushes the bottom of the petroglyph circle, continues right and brushes the bottom of the sun symbol without entering it. Meanwhile, a second sunlit point moves in, its forward tip penetrating the centers of both the circle and the sun symbols. There is also an equinox interaction on this same set of petroglyphs.
ROBERT AND ANN PRESTON

VISITING THE SALADO WORLD

BESH-BA-GOWAH ARCHAEOLOGICAL PARK

This little-known ruin, operated as a park by the town of Globe, Arizona, is one of the largest and most striking prehistoric pueblos in the Southwest. There are two added bonuses. The adjacent museum displays an excellent collection of Salado polychromes, and the pueblo is one of the rare ruins that is entirely wheelchair-friendly. When word finally filters out, this park is certain to draw more than its present 40 visitors a day.

Besh-Ba-Gowah does little to explain who or what the Salado were. The remains of a Hohokam pithouse village dating from A.D. 900 lie directly below it; the Salado pueblo was begun about 1225. Archaeologists are unsure whether the Hohokam were still around by the latter date. The stone pueblo has all the hallmarks of Mogollon architecture, including a square kiva, along with an unusual feature: a long central corridor leading from the outside past a dozen interior rooms to the central plaza.

This was apparently an important town. At its prime it comprised about 146 ground-floor and 61 second-story rooms. More than 150 burials were found under the plaza, most with elaborate accoutrements signifying their high social status.

Besh-Ba-Gowah means "Place of Metal" in Apache, a reference to the copper mines nearby. The park was opened to the public in 1988, and it is closed only on Thanksgiving, Christmas, and New Year's.

Besh-Ba-Gowah Archaeological Park, c/o City of Globe, 150 North Pine Street, Globe, AZ 85501.

(FOLLOWING PANEL) The ruins at Tonto National Monument rest in a cool, dry cliffside alcove, welcome respite from the heat of the desert. MICHAEL COLLIER

(ABOVE) The partially restored village at Besh-Ba-Gowah was originally constructed of granite cobbles, clay mortar, and pine poles. The Gila polychrome jar is an example of the impressive collection of pottery and artifacts displayed at the museum. DON B. STEVENSON
(RIGHT) One of several completed structures that were the result of the mid-1980s restoration. JERRY JACKA

TONTO NATIONAL MONUMENT

Only a handful of Salado occupied these two small but dramatic mountainside pueblos from A.D. 1250 to 1450. They lived 900 vertical feet above the artery of Salado agriculture, the Rio Salado (Salt River), a long hike down desert slopes bristling with saguaro, cholla, mesquite, and paloverde. They probably did not try to maintain crops in the fertile river basin, but instead practiced small-scale gardening and gathering on the mountain, diverting runoff onto their crops. There are 26 field houses scattered across the slopes. Since the mountainside forms an ecosystem distinct from the basin below, they likely exchanged and traded different foods with the riparian farmers.

Visitors may walk up to the lower ruin, a 16-room pueblo made of un-shaped quartzite rocks and clay-caliche mortar and plastered with mud. A National Park Service sign warns that the Salado architecture is "nondescript" because the quartzite was too hard to be fashioned into neat blocks like the favored sandstone of the Anasazi. The Park Service is overly critical. The pueblo walls exude a perfect balance between grace and strength, displayed especially in the soft morning light of spring or fall. Tonto may have been a defensive fortress, but considering the small number of occupants it more likely was a comfortable desert place to stay cool and dry for those who gardened and gathered on these hillsides. Either way, it did not lack aesthetic concern.

One of the most elegant prehistoric textiles ever discovered in the Southwest was left in this ruin: an airy cotton shirt perforated with intricately woven stepped triangles and networks of interlocking scrolls. The design is straight from Salado pottery. The shirt looks much too formal for everyday use; it must have been a ceremonial vestment.

Tonto National Monument, P.O. Box 707, Roosevelt, AZ 85545.

The dry cave that protects the ruin also helped preserve artifacts such as this woven cotton ceremonial shirt found in exceptional condition after some 700 years.
JERRY JACKA

ABANDONMENT

...A TIME TO MOVE ON

The two centuries spanning A.D. 1250 to 1450 were especially volatile and traumatic times for the people of the ancient Southwest. Imagine an upward-curling line on a graph representing the region's population, and just above it a line ominously veering downward, tracing the shrinking natural resources available to the people. Just about where they intersect, imagine a bolt of lightning suddenly appearing, shattering the deliberately arcing curves. The bolt represents the whims of the spirits, who unleashed too much rain from the sky, or perhaps withheld it, or brought winter too early and parked it on the plateaus and valleys for too long.

The consequence of all this was the phenomenon archaeologists call the "abandonment," even though the word is misleading and superficial. What happened between A.D. 1250 and 1450 is profoundly complicated. Every major culture in the Southwest either moved, collapsed, disappeared, fragmented, merged with something else, or became something new. Apparently there were many causes, most of them in dispute among furrow-browed archaeologists. No single, short-term event, such as drought, explains it. But since the 200-year bracket of time was relatively narrow, the sequence of events preceding the abandonment, like a string of kidnappings, raises the suspicion of some connection among them.

Museum exhibits typically shroud the question in mystery, contending nobody really knows why. Many writers on Southwestern archaeology fog it with hazy clichés — "worn cultural patterns ...." But the abandonment is not such a shadowy enigma. Examine what was happening at the time, apply both archaeological science and common sense, and a fairly distinct picture of the reasons for the collapse, if not the process, begins to take shape.

A visitor crossing Arizona, New Mexico, Utah, or Colorado today can sometimes drive 50 or even 100 miles between towns. This would not have been possible in A.D. 1250. While prehistoric "towns" were small, populated by only a few people up to a few thousand, they were not far apart. Population had been increasing steadily since A.D. 850, and the Southwest was teeming with people. Archaeologist Gary Matlock has estimated there were 30,000 to 40,000 Anasazi living in the southwestern corner of Colorado alone — an area today inhabited by fewer than half that many people.

Because of widespread trade and the population explosion, different cultures were mingling increasingly after A.D. 1250. Hohokam pithouses appeared in the lee of San Francisco Peaks, Anasazi pottery was being traded into the Tonto Basin, the Salado polychrome pottery cult spread into central Hohokam land, and Anasazi and Mogollon architects worked side by side in the highlands of Arizona and New Mexico.

While there was mingling, there also was trouble — an inevitable consequence of people of different ethnic stripes colliding in an increasingly crowded land.

Until recently, most archaeologists have ignored or dismissed the evidence for prehistoric "warfare" in the Southwest, but it is there nonetheless.

"Look around the world, in all of human history, and wherever you look, someone's killing someone," said archaeologist Christy Turner, a leading investigator of Anasazi warfare. "Why should you look at the Colorado Plateau and expect to see nothing but peaceful people growing beans and dancing?"

Among the earliest indications of less-than-peaceful people is the evidence of a massacre in Canyon del Muerto, a tributary of Canyon de Chelly. Sometime around A.D. 300 someone heaped a pile

of corpses in a cave, their skulls smashed with stones. The victims included babies, children, and old women as well as men. Imbedded in the ribs of one skeleton was an ominous artifact: part of the shaft and the head of an arrow. Early Basketmakers were not yet using bows and arrows, so the massacre may have been the work of invaders. On the other hand, Basketmakers were using atlatls. Atlatl "darts" had removable foreshafts

and points similar to that of later bows and arrows, only larger.

From later times, generally between A.D. 900 and 1350, Turner and others have documented hundreds of mass burials, smashed skulls, dismembered skeletons, and other signs of violence.

A prehistoric village near present-day Gallina, New Mexico, yielded dozens of skeletons with arrows and axes imbedded in them, and 49 people were found unburied on the floors of burned houses. Archaeologist Alfred E. Dittert, who worked on the Gallina excavations, agreed that aggression was not uncommon. But he felt that at Gallina and elsewhere in the Southwest they should be described more accurately as skirmishes or raids. "What happened here is a far cry from some of the early 'kills' in Europe." He added, ". . . the people in the Southwest put more energy into other things than war."

Still, the great pueblo of Paquimé (Casas Grandes) came to a dramatic end around 1400 when unknown marauders overran it, killed several hundred men, women, and children, smashed ceremonial altar pieces, burned ceiling beams that caused the city to collapse on itself, and then walked away from the carnage. Apparently they didn't loot it and they didn't bother to bury the dead . . . nor did they leave any clues.

Some early Europeans who encountered the presumed descendants of prehistoric Southwesterners wrote of historically violent practices among them. Ignaz Pfefferkorn, a Jesuit missionary who served in Sonora and present-day Arizona from 1756 to 1767, observed:

The different tribes which live in Sonora were, before the present

(ABOVE) A petroglyph illustrating eagle catching. The eagle is a powerful symbol in Pueblo cultures. In the Hopi origin tales, the eagle was the first creature the people encountered when they emerged into this world. He granted them permission to stay and told them when they wanted to send message to the creator, to use his feathers. To this day they still use eagle feathers on their *pahos*, or "prayer sticks." FRED HIRSCHMANN
(FACING PAGE) Pottery, native desert seeds, and a mortar and pestle for grinding them are remnants from the Hohokam time-of-plenty. JERRY JACKA

time, almost always at war among themselves. An unimportant incident was frequently sufficient to provoke one nation against another. Among such wild and revengeful people the war sometimes lasted until one side was either almost completely wiped out or was forced to take flight to a distant region.

Pfefferkorn frequently exaggerated, and his words here have the hint of imagined superiority — Pima Indians, after all, could have noted that Europeans were "almost always at war among themselves." However, Todd Bostwick pointed out raiding is not the equivalent of warfare, and those same tribes were also constantly engaged in alliance building and inter-marriage. As with many societies in the world today, the terms "enemy" and "ally" relate to a dynamic process.

A Native American legend offers another possible clue. The Hopi creation myth tells of their ancestors' passage through a Third World, a place where they created great cities, grew boastful and arrogant, and eventually began making war. As author Frank Waters related it in his *Book of the Hopi*:

. . . Some of them made a *patuwvota* [shield made of hide] and with their creative power made it fly through the air. On this many of the people flew to a big city, attacked it, and returned so fast no one knew where they came from. Soon the people of many cities and countries were making patuwvotas and flying on them to attack one another.

Since this evil time immediately preceded the people's emergence into their present Fourth World, it could be read as an allegorical story about the violent end of some Southwestern clans that later coalesced as the Hopi.

Whatever prehistoric "warfare" existed, it was not organized on a large scale such as the armies of Rome, the campaigns of Charlemagne, or the Crusades

brought to Europe. There were no mass communications or weapons of mass destruction. But increasing competition over dwindling natural resources, fueled by a growing population, surely created a state of frequent tension and outbreaks of violence. Pfefferkorn's "unimportant incidents" could have seemed of life-or-death importance to prehistoric people — a dispute over control of a canal or the chopping of a mesquite grove for firewood when the live trees also were needed to produce food. But because it was not large-scaled, this cultural unrest alone does not explain the regional abandonment. It does serve, however, as an indication of stress.

With so many people trying to wrest a living from the land, its natural resources were being stretched alarmingly thin. In the Sonoran Desert, firewood is a very slowly renewing fuel. Over several centuries, 20,000 to 50,000 people living in the Phoenix basin likely denuded it of trees. The Hohokam would have been pressed to acquire enough wood for heating and cooking, not to mention burial cremations and pottery firing. On the frigid Colorado Plateau, firewood would have been even more essential, and there are arid places, such as Wupatki, where trees are anything but abundant.

A dramatically changing climate was another source of stress, although this isn't as simple as it seems at first. A number of Anasazi settlements were deserted during the great drought of 1276 to 1299. That connection is clear, but there is much more. The drought made the land ready for serious erosion. The plateau's weather then shifted temporarily in favor of heavy summer rains. Ironically, that was not a boon to agriculture. Several years of raging summer thunderstorms carved more and deeper arroyos, eventually making the land unsuitable for farming. If this had not been enough to discourage the Anasazi, a period of extended winters settled over the Colorado Plateau beginning in 1325, slicing crucial days off the summer growing seasons in the higher elevations.

Between A.D. 1250 and 1400 a vast number of Pueblo people settled in the warmer Rio Grande Valley of New Mexico, which curiously had not been claimed before by sedentary people. It seems reasonable and likely that most of them were refugees from the now-inhospitable higher areas of the Colorado Plateau and the mountains of eastern Arizona. But like so many other irritating problems of the abandonment, the trail of pottery and architecture is fuzzy. Groups that made distinctive styles of pottery on the plateau apparently moved to the valley and dispersed, fusing with other groups.

Archaeologist Charles Adams of the Arizona State Museum has developed

A menacing petroglyph kachina face glowers from a cliff along the Little Colorado River, near Springerville, Arizona.
JERRY JACKA

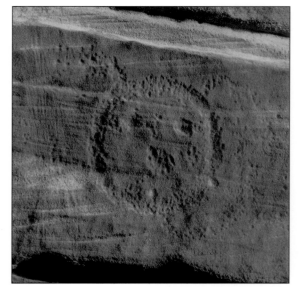

This two-horned kachina petroglyph appears near Homolovi Ruins.
LES MANEVITZ

This Tonto polychrome potshard displays a kachina face.
JERRY JACKA

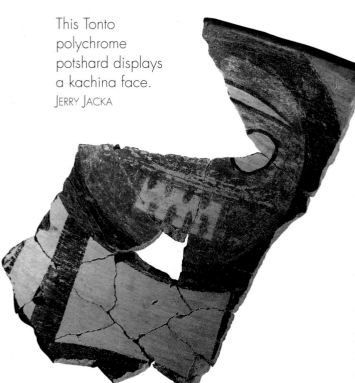

a fascinating theory in his book *The Origin and Development of the Pueblo Katsina Cult* that neatly explains how refugees of different cultures might have been able to come together in harmony. The katsina cult (popularly spelled "kachina"), which is central to Hopi and Zuni religion today, began to develop on the Colorado Plateau in the early 1300s. While kachina ceremonies were primarily associated with rain, fertility, and curing, they were also great social occasions. Other functions included the redistribution of food to families, the acting as disciplinarian to children, and helping to organize community work such as the annual clearing of springs.

Kachinas are not gods; they are ancestor-spirits serving as messengers between the Pueblo people and their gods. In modern Hopi life, they appear both in the form of dolls traditionally made for young Hopi children (and more recently for sale to collectors) and as masked dancers who stage elaborate,

Kachinas, spirit messengers to the gods, are important symbols in Pueblo Indian religion today. Their masklike images began appearing in petroglyphs, pottery, and kiva murals throughout the Four Corners region in the early 1300s.
(ABOVE) Kachina murals in the kiva at Kuaua Ruin, Coronado State Monument, New Mexico. Modern Pueblo Indians say the panels symbolically portray numerous aspects of Anasazi religion. For example: Yellow Corn Maiden *Kochininako*, fire god *Shulawitsi*, the rattlesnake and eagle (both messengers for rain), various ceremonies, the universe, and the history of their peoples' emergence into this world.
JERRY JACKA

159

specialization of labor, more apparent class division, and more hostile feelings. Government became more complex and more centralized — it had to in order to build and maintain public works such as the Hohokam canals — and so it had more of an investment in the status quo. Small clusters of a few families could have migrated easily, seeking fresh resources. But prehistoric towns would have been slower to respond, and that could have invited ecological disaster.

Disease may have invaded the towns precisely because they were towns. Given prehistoric sanitation, this made them more vulnerable to epidemics. Wupatki pueblo may have been a tragic example. Thirty-one people were discovered in a mass burial in one room. Archaeologist Christy Turner has closely examined their remains and declares there is no evidence of violent death. Disease, he concludes, is the only

apart; the center cannot hold." An ancient Navajo belief is more specific: The "enemy ancestors" vanished because they "began to do and learn things beyond the knowledge that was set for them."

Another prophetic line written about our modern Southwest appeared in Lawrence Clark Powell's 1976 bicentennial history of Arizona. Our most pressing problem, Powell wrote, "is that of a rising flood of people into a land naturally unsuited to large numbers of people." Around A.D. 1250, at the peak of their success and ambition, prehistoric Southwesterners thought they were solving that problem. They would not be the last to cherish that belief.

growing seasons.
TOM DANIELSEN

(BELOW)
A scattering of pottery shards and corncobs creates a trash midden mosaic at Keet Seel Ruin, Navajo National Monument.
LARRY ULRICH

highly structured ceremonies. In prehistoric times, just as now, to make a village function efficiently all segments had to work together for the good of the whole. And here is where the kachina cult played its important cross-cultural role. While clans in and of themselves tend to be divisive elements in a society, many aspects of kachina ceremonialism involve interclan cooperation. Thus the kachina cult bonded together many who were immigrants from divergent social and political backgrounds.

Apparently the cult functioned well, because by the 1400s it had spread as far as the Rio Grande valley of New Mexico. Dramatic kiva murals depicting kachinas have been found in 15th-century Hopi villages and at Kuaua Pueblo Ruins north of Albuquerque. "The cult allowed aggregation by encouraging cooperative networks," wrote Adams. "Without aggregation . . . it is likely that settlements established in the late 13th and early 14th centuries would have remained unstable . . . and that conflict would have developed over land ownership." Adam's book makes another rather poignant observation: "The first choice for leadership was not conflict, but the avoidance of conflict."

Climate was also a likely coconspira-

in A.D. 1358 and 1380 to '82 is confirmed by tree ring data from mountain watersheds. But there is evidence that the Hohokam were already in trouble by that time.

Archaeologist Alfred E. Dittert observed that the climate change that began in 1325 had replaced the up-till-then summer-dominant moisture pattern with one that was winter-dominant. This continued more than 500 years until 1850 and typically caused longer winters in the mountains, continuously running rivers that choked the great Hohokam canals with silt all summer, and when rains were needed most to bring crops to harvest, there were none.

Archaeologists who excavated villages around Pueblo Grande in Phoenix analyzed the plant pollen and found that between A.D. 1100 and 1450, the people were increasingly dependent on wild desert plants and less on agriculture. The Hohokam had always supplemented farming with gathering, but as their population grew, they needed to become more reliant on agriculture, not less. Archaeologists examined 600 burials from the two centuries before 1450 and found evidence of serious malnutrition in the bones. Women developed osteoporosis as soon as they were of childbearing age and had it for the rest of

WHEN VISITING
THE PREHISTORIC WORLD

Visiting every park and monument that preserves Southwestern prehistory would take months and cover thousands of miles of Arizona, New Mexico, Colorado, Utah, and Mexico highways and back roads. This is not a discouraging prospect. Quite to the contrary, immersion in the prehistoric world is the best way to begin understanding it, and may lead to a lifelong fascination. And, incidentally, it comprises some of North America's most extravagant natural landscapes.

Where possible, visit at sunrise or sunset. The usual crowds are absent, and the soft light and deep shadows accent colors and enhance the drama of the architecture. Some sites, such as Hovenweep National Monument in Utah, have no gates and are open during all daylight hours; others restrict visitors to 8 A.M. to 5 P.M. hours. Spring and fall are the best times for visits. Winters are cold and summers bring crowds.

Wherever a park ranger offers a talk or guided tour, take advantage: the rangers know more than the park brochures tell. Some have university degrees in archaeology. Unless prohibited, take time to explore the environs around a ruin. Try to understand its relationships to water sources, the sun's arc through the sky, and where crops were cultivated. Binoculars and a compass will help. Watch for unadvertised petroglyphs, plant life, small game, and snakes.

Observe archaeological etiquette and the law. Never climb on walls or touch rock art. If you find a potsherd or lithic — a stone tool or projectile point — leave it. Take photographs, not souvenirs. In archaeology, context is vital. A pot on a collector's private mantle has little value to science, but that pot studied in the context of its ancient trash mound will tell archaeologists how and when it may have been used. The U.S. Archaeological Resources Protection Act of 1979 prohibits removing or defacing artifacts on federal lands; most states have similar laws regarding state lands. Tragically, these laws came too late for thousands of prehistoric settlements. The stories they might have told were lost to pothunters generations ago.

(**ABOVE**) A visitor and Ute Indian guide examine a kiva in Ute Mountain Tribal Park, Colorado.
TOM BEAN
(**RIGHT**) Winter sunrise warms Hovenweep National Monument.
(**FOLLOWING PANEL**) View from the visitors' overlook into Canyon del Muerto, Canyon de Chelly National Monument, provides a bird's-eye perspective of Antelope House Ruin.
BOTH BY TOM DANIELSEN

ROCK ART

On a warm spring day west of the Arizona desert town of Gila Bend, an *Arizona Highways* editor and some friends stared together at a picture pecked in a rock perhaps 10 centuries past. Showing a photograph of that rock to a Hopi friend some weeks later brought a startled response: "That's my name!"

The petroglyph depicted a cross-hatched object rising vertically out of a field of wavy lines. It meant nothing special to the editor. The Hopi read it as "corn-standing-in-water," which was indeed his name.

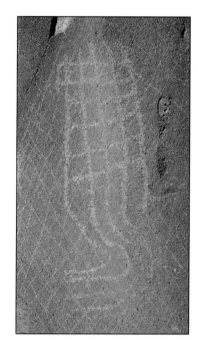

Petroglyph interpreted as corn standing in water.
WESLEY HOLDEN

The moment was filled with insight. The white man was reminded of the ancient roots of Hopi culture in Arizona, and the profound importance of cultivated corn in the life of Native Americans. It also made him wonder about the possibility that rock art had been intended to communicate across the chasm of centuries. Was it?

Archaeologist Boma Johnson, in Yuma, Arizona, told of taking a flock of seventh graders on a field trip up the Colorado River to study prehistoric drawings. When they came across an image of a human figure without legs, a Hispanic boy asked, "What's that?" His 12-year-old Indian companion answered, "A spirit."

"How do you know that?" the Hispanic asked. "Because spirits don't need legs to walk," replied the Indian.

For the archaeologist, that adolescent revelation suggested a tradition that has spanned at least 2,000 years and scores of different cultures. Perhaps rock art was (and is) a highly expressive *lingua franca*, a vocabulary of metaphorical symbols that once was understood by all Native Americans who shared a profound knowledge of the natural world.

Other archaeologists scoff at this idea. As they point out, tests have been conducted in which the same set of rock art motifs has been submitted to a number of different Indians. There were as many interpretations as there were "readers." Perhaps the only completely safe statement about rock art today is that non-Indians agree even less about its meaning.

The arid Southwest has an abundance of exposed rocks — hillside boulders, escarpments, canyon walls — ideal settings that seem to have encouraged a prehistoric explosion in rock art. Granting a few exceptions (notably Australia), nowhere in the world is there such a profusion of rock art.

Scholars and connoisseurs make important distinction among several forms: "petroglyphs" are scratched or pecked on stone, and "pictographs" are painted. Both are found in the Southwest, but petroglyphs are much more common. A third form, even more baffling, is the "geoglyph," a term given them by archaeologist Boma Johnson. They are huge pictures made by clearing the desert floor of pebbles or aligning large stones into figures best seen by hawks and eagles.

What was rock art intended to communicate? Many different things, probably, just as modern books span a world of functions. A phone book is altogether different from this book, yet the two use the same 26 letters and 10 numerals, and might lie on the same table together — two facts that should baffle the archaeologist of the distant future who finds them in a dig. Rock art is no different.

Perhaps it related to hunting, agriculture, rain, human fertility, indicated clan migrations, or recorded a census. Or perhaps the drawings represented spirits invoked by priests during ritual ceremonies, creation stories, or were mnemonic devices. Some petroglyphs definitely charted the seasons, precisely marking summer solstice, winter solstice, and equinox — when to plant, when to have ceremonies. Some were clearly trail indicators, and others recorded events. Archaeologists are certain of at least one event, the supernova of A.D. 1054, which was drawn in an accurate position relative to the moon in several petroglyphs and pictographs in Arizona and New Mexico.

Some rock art researchers wield Occam's razor to help interpret the drawings: this is the principle that says the most obvious explanation of something is the most likely to be correct. But religion and cosmology in the prehistoric Southwest were anything but simple. When a prehistoric artist scratched drawings of scorpions onto hillside boulders, the obvious interpretation is that he was recording the natural world around his people. A Modern Zuni, however, interpreted petroglyphs of poisonous creatures as an ancestral intent to sting his people's enemies.

In prehistoric art, obvious explanations should trigger one's caution light. But the fun of studying petroglyphs is that a nonprofessional may have an idea just as good as an archaeologist.

(ABOVE) An aerial view of the "racetrack" geoglyph along the Gila River in southwestern Arizona.
WESLEY HOLDEN

(FOLLOWING PANEL) Pictograph handprints embellish Sunflower Cave
in Canyon de Chelly National Monument.
DAVID MUENCH

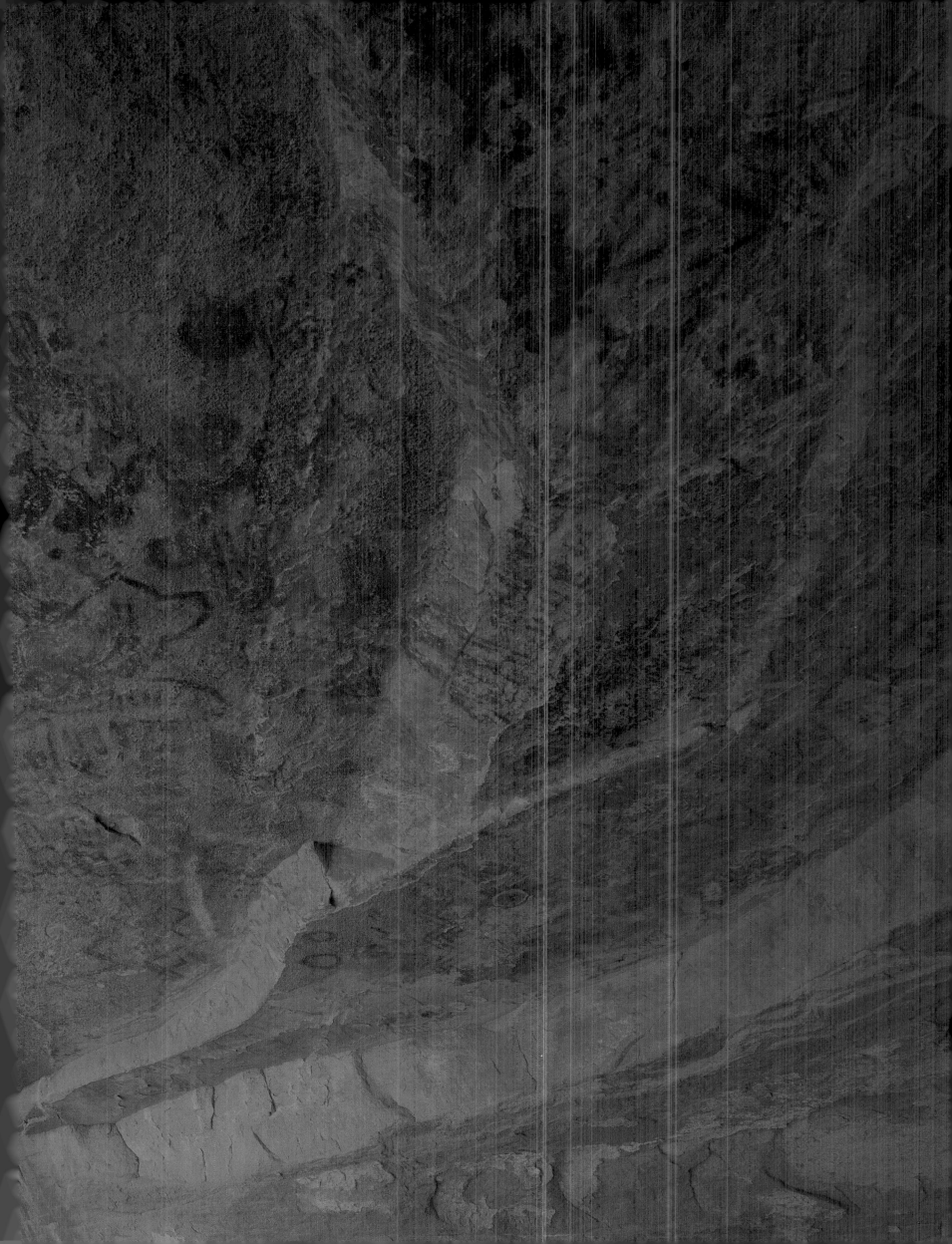

MUSEUMS

Warning: Southwestern archaeology is addictive. An amateur enthusiast exploring the fascinating prehistory of the Southwest can sift among scores of museum exhibits, interpretive programs, and study trips. The following is a selective list.

Every March is Arizona Archaeology Month. More than 100 exhibits, lectures, and tours are offered at museums and archaeological sites around the state. Most are free, some are especially for children. For a brochure of events, contact: State Historic Preservation Office, Arizona State Parks, 1300 West Washington, Phoenix, AZ 85007.

The Arizona State Museum at the University of Arizona in Tucson was founded in 1893, 19 years before Arizona became a state. It holds Arizona's largest research collection of prehistoric artifacts, although only a fraction are on public display. The museum library, directly across the university mall, has a vast collection of archaeological books, periodicals, and papers, and it is open to the public. Arizona State Museum, University of Arizona, Tucson AZ 85721.

A Hohokam red-on-buff bowl on display at Arizona State Museum on the campus of the University of Arizona, Tucson.
DAVID MUENCH

The Museum of Northern Arizona in Flagstaff has constructed a reproduction of a kiva and murals from the Hopi village of Awatovi.
JERRY JACKA

The Museum of Northern Arizona was founded in 1928 by archaeologist Harold S. Colton and the irritated residents of Flagstaff. It seems that the Smithsonian Institution was excavating Elden Pueblo, a Sinagua village just east of the town, and residents were watching trainloads of prehistoric Arizona being shipped back East. The museum was created to research and exhibit the natural history and archaeology of the Colorado Plateau, which today it does extraordinarily well. It offers an excellent archaeological exhibit, at least a dozen "ventures" (extended field trips) every year, and a quarterly magazine, *Plateau*, for members. The museum library, open to the public, has indexed not only its collection of books but also decades of archaeological papers and articles — a unique and useful research tool. Museum of Northern Arizona, Route 4, Box 720, Flagstaff, AZ 86001.

While the Museum of Northern Arizona emphasizes science, The Heard Museum of Phoenix focuses on the arts of Native Americans and aboriginal cultures worldwide. The museum was founded in 1929 by Dwight and Maie Bartlett Heard to house their personal collection and today enjoys international fame. Rotating art shows join "Native Peoples of the Southwest," the permanent prehistory exhibit. The Heard also has a library and sponsors several field trips every year. Heard Museum, 22 East Monte Vista Road, Phoenix, AZ 85004.

The Museum of New Mexico actually comprises four separate Santa Fe museums exhibiting art from the ancient world to the contemporary. Archaeology enthusiasts should visit the Museum of Indian Arts and Culture, which houses a

This *Pahlik Mana* (butterfly maiden) Hopi kachina doll is part of The Heard Museum's Barry Goldwater Collection.
JERRY JACKA

magnificent collection of pottery spanning more than a thousand years. Free docent-guided lecture tours are enlightening. Museum of Indian Arts and Culture, 710 Camino Lejo, Santa Fe, NM 87501.

The Amerind Foundation is the vision of one of those Easterners who came to the Southwest, became bewitched by its ancient past, and gave up a prospering business career to devote his life to archaeology. William S. Fulton created the nonprofit research institution in 1937 on his Texas Canyon ranch 60 miles east of Tucson. Among other things, the museum features an amazing collection of effigy vessels excavated at Paquimé (Casas Grandes) in Chihuahua, Mexico. Take the Dragoon Exit from Interstate 10 (Exit 318) and drive one mile southeast. Amerind Foundation, P.O. Box 248, Dragoon, AZ 85609.

The Anasazi Heritage Center in Colorado is the newest and most comprehensive Anasazi museum. Among its attractions are a reconstruction of a prehistoric face, a full-size replica of a pithouse, and a fascinating Anasazi bowl decorated with paintings of women wearing squash-blossom hairdos — a style that endured among the Hopi into the 20th century. The museum, operated by the U.S. Bureau of Land Management, is situated on the slope of a hill overlooking Montezuma Valley. It is located on Colorado Highway 184 three miles west of Dolores. Anasazi Heritage Center, 27501 Highway 184, Dolores, CO 81323.

Polychrome human effigy pots from Casas Grandes Ruins can be seen at the Amerind Foundation, Dragoon, Arizona. JACK DYKINGA

Crow Canyon Archaeological Center, a not-for-profit research and educational foundation, offers a wide variety of archaeological and cultural programs, most lasting a week. Several programs include not only visits to ruins but actual excavating. Crow Canyon Archaeological Center, 23390 County Road K, Cortez, CO 81321.

White Mesa Institute for Cultural Studies offers several educational field trips in the Four Corners region every year, all led by prominent archaeologists. The institute is run by the San Juan campus of the College of Eastern Utah. White Mesa Institute, P.O. Box 211248, Salt Lake City, UT 84121.

Known worldwide for its collections of prehistoric and modern Indian art, The Heard Museum in downtown Phoenix was founded by Phoenix pioneers Dwight and Maie Bartlett Heard. JERRY JACKA

INDEX

Standard type indicates a text
reference.
Numbers followed by an "m"
are a map reference.
Boldface denotes a photograph.

(LEFT) Autumn brushes the aspens
with gold below Betatakin Ruin,
Navaho National Monument.
TOM ALGIRE

ACKNOWLEDGMENTS

Many professional archaeologists, amateur enthusiasts, institutions, and businesses big and small generously gave their time and expertise to the author during the research for this book. Sincere thanks to: Christopher Adams, John Blackwell, Todd Bostwick, Cory Breternitz, Patricia Cheek, Gerold Collings, Patricia Crown, Alfred E. Dittert, Christian Downum, Paul Fish, Bernard Fontana, Dorothy House, Boma Johnson, Dennis and Janis Lyon, James Officer, Carol Patterson-Rudolph, Robert and Ann Preston, Glen Rice, Chris Robinson, Raymond Tom, Christy Turner, R. Gwinn Vivian, P.K. Weis, and David R. Wilcox.

Arizona Department of Transportation, Arizona State Museum, Arizona State Parks, Arizona State University Anthropology Department, Besh-Ba-Gowah Archaeological Park, The Heard Museum, Jet Propulsion Laboratory, Museum of Northern Arizona, National Park Service, National Park Service Western Archaeology Center, Northern Arizona

FURTHER READING

For further reading, *Prehistory of the Southwest* by Linda S. Cordell (Academic Press, Orlando, 1984) is an authoritative and comprehensive book on Southwestern archaeology. *Those Who Came Before* by Robert H. and Florence C. Lister (University of Arizona Press, Tucson, 1983) is an engaging but not overly detailed survey.

Enemy Ancestors by Gary Matlock (Northland Press, Flagstaff, 1988) is a popular overview of the Anasazi culture. *The Hohokam: Ancient People of the Desert* (School of American Research Press, Santa Fe, 1991) edited by David Grant Noble is a very readable anthology on the Hohokam.

A Field Guide to Rock Art Symbols by Alex Patterson (Johnson Books, Boulder, 1992) offers possible interpretations of rock art, indexed by subject (hunting, spirals, snakes, etc.). *Indian Rock Art of the Southwest* by Polly Schaafsma (University of New Mexico Press, Albuquerque, 1986). Although of an academic nature this is the largest and most comprehensive study of the subject.

Generations in Clay by Alfred E. Dittert and Fred Plog (Northland Press, Flagstaff, 1980) is a photographically illustrated, detailed guide to Pueblo pottery art from Anasazi to modern Santa Clara. *The Origin and Development of the Pueblo Katsina Cult* by E. Charles Adams (University of Arizona Press, Tucson, 1991) contains much scientifically presented information. It is one of the most insightful books on the subject written to date.

Additionally, thousands of books and papers on Southwestern prehistory are held in: Arizona State Museum, Tucson; Hayden Library at Arizona State University, Tempe; Heard Museum, Phoenix; Museum of Northern Arizona, Flagstaff; and Museum of New Mexico libraries, which are accessible to everyone.

(ABOVE) A 4,000-year-old split-twig figure of a mountain sheep from the archaic culture was found in northern Arizona. JERRY JACKA

(RIGHT) Signatures from the past. Anasazi pictographs of handprints painted on the walls of a cave in Canyon del Muerto. GEORGE H.H. HUEY